From Your Friends At **The MAILBOX**®

OCTOBER

A MONTH OF REPRODUCIBLES AT YOUR FINGERTIPS!

Grades 4–5

Senior Editor:
Thad H. McLaurin

Associate Editor:
Cindy Mondello

Writers:
Julie Alarie, Therese Durhman, Rusty Fischer,
Peggy W. Hambright, Thad H. McLaurin,
Cindy Mondello, Gail Peckumn, Connie Ramey,
Patricia Twohey, Stephanie Willett-Smith

Art Coordinator:
Clevell Harris

Artists:
Teresa Davidson, Nick Greenwood, Clevell Harris,
Sheila Krill, Rob Mayworth, Kimberly Richard, Barry Slate

Cover Artist:
Jennifer Tipton Bennett

Manufactured in the United States

10 9 8 7 6 5 4 3 2 1

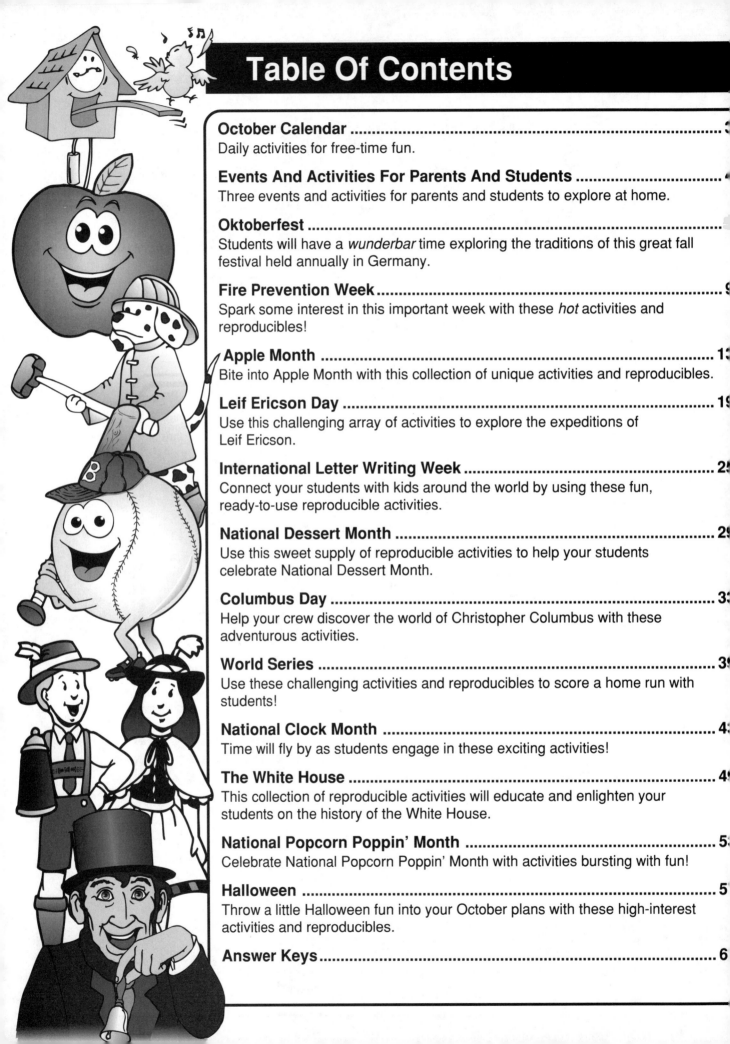

Table Of Contents

Name _____

October Free Time

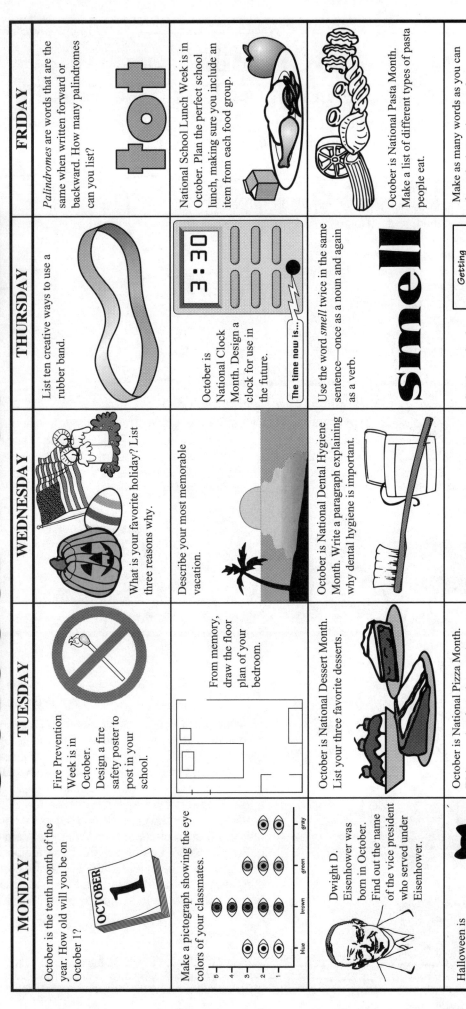

MONDAY	TUESDAY	WEDNESDAY	THURSDAY	FRIDAY
October is the tenth month of the year. How old will you be on October 1?	Fire Prevention Week is in October. Design a fire safety poster to post in your school.	What is your favorite holiday? List three reasons why.	List ten creative ways to use a rubber band.	*Palindromes* are words that are the same when written forward or backward. How many palindromes can you list?
Make a pictograph showing the eye colors of your classmates.	From memory, draw the floor plan of your bedroom.	Describe your most memorable vacation.	October is National Clock Month. Design a clock for use in the future. The time now is...	National School Lunch Week is in October. Plan the perfect school lunch, making sure you include an item from each food group.
Dwight D. Eisenhower was born in October. Find out the name of the vice president who served under Eisenhower.	October is National Dessert Month. List your three favorite desserts.	October is National Dental Hygiene Month. Write a paragraph explaining why dental hygiene is important.	Use the word *smell* twice in the same sentence—once as a noun and again as a verb.	October is National Pasta Month. Make a list of different types of pasta people eat.
Halloween is celebrated on October 31. List five rules children should follow to ensure their safety while trick-or-treating.	October is National Pizza Month. Write a recipe for a dessert pizza.	**31** October has 31 days. List the other months of the year that have 31 days.	Get Organized Week is October 6–12. Develop a five-point written plan to improve your organization. *Getting Organized* 1. ___ 2. ___ 3. ___ 4. ___ 5. ___	Make as many words as you can from the letters in *pumpkin*.

©1999 The Education Center, Inc. • *October Monthly Reproducibles* • Grades 4–5 • TEC962

Note To The Teacher: Have each student staple a copy of this page in a file folder. Direct students to store their completed work inside their folders.

3

OCTOBER
Events And Activities For The Family

Directions: Select at least one activity below to complete as a family by the end of October. *(Challenge: See if your family can complete all three activities.)*

Fire Prevention Week

Fire Prevention Week is held during the week of October 9 in remembrance of the Great Chicago Fire of 1871. Explain to your family that the Chicago fire destroyed 17,430 buildings and caused 196 million dollars' worth of damage! Discuss the safety procedures to follow in case a fire occurs in your home. Then have each family member draw a floor plan of your house and plot an escape route to use in the event of a fire. Walk through each route to determine which is the fastest, and adopt the winner as your family's new escape route!

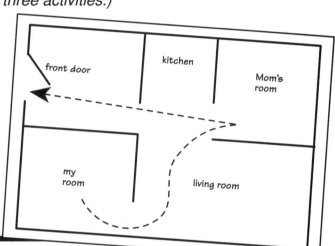

Kindness Is Contagious!

Sweetest Day (celebrated on the third Saturday in October) began when a resident of Cleveland, Ohio, decided to help some of the underprivileged in his community. He delivered small gifts to orphans and shut-ins. The idea soon spread. Celebrate Sweetest Day by having each member of the family secretly draw another family member's name from a hat. Whether it's fetching Dad's slippers or making Mom dessert, do whatever you can to show that person special kindness for the entire day.

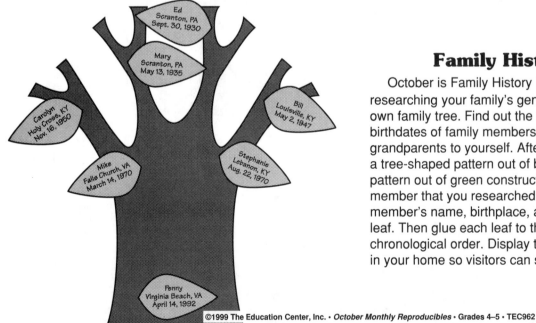

Family History Month

October is Family History Month. Celebrate by researching your family's genealogy and creating your own family tree. Find out the names, birthplaces, and birthdates of family members, dating from your great-grandparents to yourself. After collecting all the data, cut a tree-shaped pattern out of brown paper. Cut one leaf pattern out of green construction paper for each family member that you researched. Write each family member's name, birthplace, and birthdate on a separate leaf. Then glue each leaf to the tree in the correct chronological order. Display the tree in a prominent place in your home so visitors can see your family pride!

©1999 The Education Center, Inc. • *October Monthly Reproducibles* • Grades 4–5 • TEC962

Note To The Teacher: Distribute one copy of this page to each student at the beginning of October. Encourage each family to complete at least one activity by the end of the month.

4

Oktoberfest

The first Oktoberfest was held on October 17, 1810, to honor the wedding of the future King Louis I of Bavaria. Since then, this fall festival has been held annually, bringing tourists from all over the world to share the best of food, drink, and entertainment. The festival is now held from mid-September into October.

Oompah-Pah Polka

The delightful music played by the Bavarian bands during Oktoberfest gets everyone in a festive mood. Get your students feeling "Oktoberfest-ive" by teaching them the following song, sung to the tune of "The Beer Barrel Polka" ("Roll out the barrel…").

Now it's October.
We think October is best.
We love October!
We're having an Oktoberfest.
Sing, dance, be merry.
Tell us an October jest.
Now's the time for celebrating.
It's OKTOBERFEST!

"Oktober-feast"

Not only are Germans known for being hardworking and disciplined, but they are also famous for their love of good food. Enjoy a sampling of some of this good food by planning an "Oktober-feast." Invite parents or other classes to sample German foods and enjoy German music (see "Oompah-Pah Polka"). Prepare your feast with the following foods: root beer (served in paper steins from "Design A Stein"), frankfurters, sauerkraut, German mustard, pumpernickel bread or rolls, strudel, and *Himmel Und Erde* (see recipe).

Himmel Und Erde
Heaven And Earth

Ingredients:
4 medium potatoes, cut into 1-inch cubes
2 apples, sliced
1 tablespoon sugar
4 slices bacon, cut into 1-inch pieces
1 medium onion, sliced
1 tablespoon butter, softened
dash of nutmeg
salt

Directions:
Place potatoes, apples, and sugar in one inch of boiling, salted water. Return to a boil. Reduce heat. Cover and cook 10 to 15 minutes, until tender. Drain. Meanwhile, fry bacon and drain on paper towels. Cook onion in the same pan as the bacon. Place the potatoes and apples in a serving dish. Dot with butter, then sprinkle with nutmeg. Top with onion and bacon. Makes four to six servings.

Design A Stein

The *stein,* a large earthenware mug, has become one of the many symbols of Oktoberfest. Bring in samples or pictures of steins to show your class how they are decorated. Then set up a Stein Design Center in a corner of your classroom. Place a supply of paper beverage cups with handles, colored markers, and pictures or samples of a variety of steins in the center. Then invite students to visit the center and create their own steins.

Oktoberfest: vocabulary

Directions: Use a German dictionary to find a word that begins with each letter in October. Write each word and its definition in the appropriate spaces, then illustrate each word in the appropriate box.

O	C	T	O	B	E	R
(word)	(word)	(word)	(word)	(word)	(word)	(word)

Note To The Teacher: Divide students into groups of three or four. Give each student in each group one copy of this page. Also give each group one German dictionary. Instruct the students in each group to work together to complete the reproducible as directed.

 **"Oktober-quest"**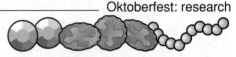

Just how much do you know about the month of October? Check your October IQ by researching the answers to each question in the treasure chests below. Record each answer in the appropriate treasure chest.

1. On October 2, 1950, the first PEANUTS® comic strip was published. Who is the creator of Charlie Brown®, Snoopy®, and the gang?

2. October 5, 1882, is the birthday of the "father of the space age." What is his name?

3. The first lady of the United States from 1933 to 1945 was born on October 11, 1884. What was her name?

4. On October 14, Chuck Yeager flew faster than the speed of sound while test-piloting an XS-1 aircraft. In what year did this event occur?

5. On October 14, 1964, Martin Luther King, Jr., received a special award. What was this award?

6. October 15 is National Grouch Day. Who is Oscar the Grouch®?

7. October 16 is Noah Webster's birthdate. You have read (at least part of) an updated version of the book he wrote. What type of reference book is he known for writing?

8. Alaska Day is October 18. It celebrates the transfer of Alaska to U.S. control. Which country had control of Alaska before the United States?

9. The man who developed the polio vaccine was born on October 28, 1914. What was his name?

Bonus Box: On the back of this page, write an "Oktober-jest"—a joke or riddle about October.

©1999 The Education Center, Inc. • *October Monthly Reproducibles* • Grades 4–5 • TEC962 • Key p. 63

Note To The Teacher: Duplicate one copy of this page for each student. Supply the class with a variety of resource materials.

Ready For Oktoberfest

Four cousins, Lester, Chester, Hester, and Ester, went to the Oktoberfest celebration Saturday. Each cousin ate his or her favorite Oktoberfest food and wore his or her favorite clothing.

Directions: Read the clues below to find out each cousin's favorite food and clothing. Mark the grid using a ✓ if there is a match and an ✗ if there is not.

1. Lester is wearing *lederhosen,* but does not like to eat pumpernickel bread or sauerkraut.

2. Chester is not wearing an embroidered apron.

3. The cousin who wears an embroidered apron does not eat sauerkraut or strudel, but the cousin who eats frankfurters wears hiking boots.

4. Ester enjoys the tartness of sauerkraut.

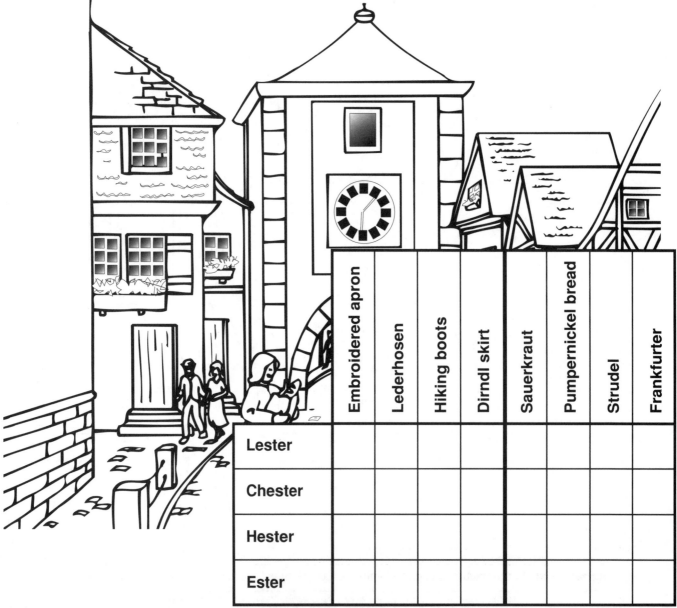

	Embroidered apron	Lederhosen	Hiking boots	Dirndl skirt	Sauerkraut	Pumpernickel bread	Strudel	Frankfurter
Lester								
Chester								
Hester								
Ester								

FIRE PREVENTION WEEK

Fire Prevention Week is celebrated each fall during the week of October 9. It was during the week of October 9, 1871, that the Great Chicago Fire occurred, destroying 17,430 buildings and causing 196 million dollars' worth of damage.

Tools Of The Trade

Spark interest in fire fighting and review simple machines with the following activity. Have students brainstorm a list of tools used by firefighters. Then have them determine which simple machines (inclined plane, wedge, screw, pulley, lever, and wheel and axle) make up each tool. (See page 63 for definitions of each type of simple machine.) Next divide your students into pairs. Give each pair one sheet of drawing paper and crayons or markers. Challenge each pair to design a new piece of fire-fighting equipment that makes use of one or more of the six types of simple machines. Have each pair share its design with the rest of the class and describe the design, its purpose, and how it works.

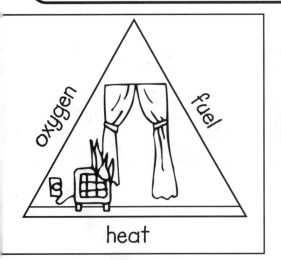

Triangle Of Fire

Ignite enthusiasm for fire prevention as you teach your students about the *fire triangle.* Tell students that the fire triangle refers to the three things needed to create a fire—*oxygen, fuel,* and *heat.* Inform students that removing just one of the three elements can prevent a fire or sometimes even stop a fire after it has started. Share examples of ways fires can start and have your students identify the heat source, oxygen source, and fuel source in each example. Then have students explain the easiest way to have prevented each fire. Next give each student one sheet of drawing paper. Instruct the student to draw a large triangle in the center of his paper; then write each element—fuel, heat, oxygen—along the outside of the triangle. Have the student illustrate a type of fire on the inside of the triangle, such as a space heater catching a set of curtains on fire. Have each student share his triangle of fire with the rest of the class; then post the triangles on a bulletin board titled "Triangles Of Fire."

Fire Escape

Use this fun game to help reinforce basic fire safety tips and precautions. Divide students into groups of four. Give each group one copy of page 10 and one copy of page 11, one envelope, a pair of scissors, and one game marker for each member. Instruct each team to cut apart the cards on page 11 and place them in the envelope. Have each player number himself either 1, 2, 3, or 4. Have Player 2 draw a card from the envelope and read the question to Player 1. If Player 1 answers correctly, he moves his game marker the stated number of spaces on the drawn card. If he answers incorrectly, he does not get to move ahead. Next, have Player 3 draw a card and read the question to Player 2. Continue the process until a player has escaped the building and is declared the winner. If a group runs out of cards before a winner is declared, have the group put the cards back into the envelope to be played again.

Fire Escape

You're caught in a burning building. Be the first to escape!

Note To The Teacher: Use with "Fire Escape" on page 9 and the game cards on page 11.

Fire Escape Game Cards

Q: 100 x 50 people are killed in house fires each year. How many people is that? **A:** 5,000 **Move ahead 2 spaces.**	**Q:** Should smoke detector batteries be replaced every month or every year? **A:** every year **Move ahead 3 spaces.**	**Q:** What do most people who die in fires specifically die from? **A:** smoke inhalation **Move ahead 4 spaces.**	**Q:** Name one of the three most important places to keep a home fire extinguisher. **A:** kitchen, garage, or shop **Move ahead 2 spaces.**
Q: Why should you know two ways to get out of every room in your house in case of fire? **A:** If one way is blocked, the other way can be used. **Move ahead 3 spaces.**	**Q:** Families should have a designated meeting place outside of the house in the event of a fire. Tell a good place for your family to meet. **A:** Accept any reasonable answer. **Move ahead 2 spaces.**	**Q:** Why might it be a better idea to crawl out of your house than to walk if it's on fire? **A:** Smoke and heat rise, so the area close to the floor will be cooler and contain less smoke. **Move ahead 4 spaces.**	**Q:** Within 5 minutes of the start of a fire, the ceiling can be 1000°F, where as the floor is only 90°F. Why is it hotter near the ceiling? **A:** Hot air rises. **Move ahead 3 spaces.**
Q: Within 5 minutes of the start of a fire, the temperature at eye level is 600°F, and it's 90°F at floor level. What's the difference between these two temperatures? **A:** 510 degrees **Move ahead 2 spaces.**	**Q:** Why do you think fire safety experts recommend you sleep with your bedroom door shut? **A:** If your door is shut, the fire will not spread to your room as quickly. **Move ahead 3 spaces.**	**Q:** Why is it important for fireplaces to have a screen or door? **A:** so sparks won't escape and possibly start a fire **Move ahead 2 spaces.**	**Q:** Name at least one thing that shouldn't be stored by your furnace. **A:** rags, papers, magazines, gas, or anything that can catch on fire easily **Move ahead 2 spaces.**
Q: Tell a good safety tip involving electrical outlets that could be helpful in preventing a fire. **A:** Don't overload outlets; check for loose wires; check for exposed wires; etc. **Move ahead 4 spaces.**	**Q:** Why is baking soda sometimes thrown on small kitchen fires? **A:** Water should never be thrown on a grease or an electrical fire. Baking soda will smother the flames by blocking off oxygen. **Move ahead 3 spaces.**	**Q:** Name one way young children often start fires. **A:** playing with matches or lighters **Move ahead 2 spaces.**	**Q:** Why is it especially dangerous for a person to smoke in bed? **A:** He could fall asleep and his cigarette could catch the bedding on fire. **Move ahead 2 spaces.**
Q: Why do you think it is suggested that people not wear loose-fitting clothing when they are cooking on the stove? **A:** Clothing could brush across a burner and catch on fire. **Move ahead 4 spaces.**	**Q:** Tell a dangerous place to put a real Christmas tree in your house. **A:** in front of a heat register, close to a stove, close to a fireplace, close to a space heater (accept any reasonable answer) **Move ahead 3 spaces.**	**Q:** A smoke alarm just went off while you were sleeping and you need to get out of your house quickly. Tell exactly how you would get out of your house. **A:** Accept any reasonable answer. **Move ahead 4 spaces.**	**Q:** If you catch on fire, why should you "Stop, Drop, and Roll"? **A:** to smother the flames **Move ahead 4 spaces.**
Q: If a smoke alarm went off and you ran to your bedroom door to get out, but the door felt very hot, what should you do? **A:** Try to find another escape route, such as through a window. (Don't open the door.) **Move ahead 3 spaces.**	**Q:** What does it mean when a smoke detector starts making a chirping sound? **A:** that its batteries need to be replaced **Move ahead 2 spaces.**	**Q:** A fire started in a pot left simmering on a burner. A lid is quickly put on top of the pot and the fire soon goes out. Why? **A:** The oxygen supply is cut off. **Move ahead 3 spaces.**	**Q:** Tell a specific place you have seen a fire extinguisher. **A:** Accept any reasonable answer. **Move ahead 2 spaces.**

©1999 The Education Center, Inc. • *October Monthly Reproducibles* • Grades 4–5 • TEC962

Note To The Teacher: Use with "Fire Escape" on page 9 and the gameboard on page 10.

Home Safe Home

Sparky can't make heads nor tails out of the floor plans below. He wants to make sure that smoke detectors are put in the best places. Help Sparky get started by correctly labeling each room using the clues below. Then use the floor plan to help you complete the questions and activities at the bottom of the page.

Clues:

1. Bedroom #1 is 106 sq. ft.
2. Bedroom #2 is 210 sq. ft.
3. Bedroom #3 is 115 sq. ft.
4. The kitchen is 154 sq. ft.
5. The family room is about 360 sq. ft.
6. The dining room is 98 sq. ft.
7. The living room is 77 sq. ft.
8. The utility room is 90 sq. ft.
9. The last two rooms are bathrooms. How many square feet is each bathroom? _____

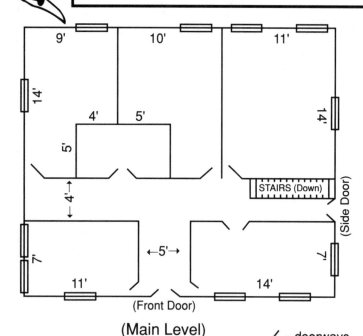

(Main Level)

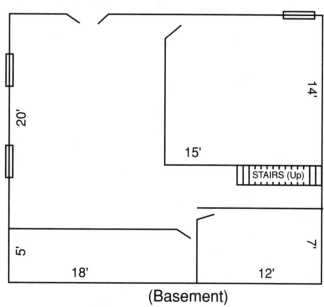

(Basement)

___/ = doorways   [===] = windows

Questions And Activities:

1. Put at least one smoke detector on every level and outside each bedroom. Use this symbol to label each smoke detector on the floor plan above.

2. A house should contain one fire extinguisher for every 600 square feet of living space. What is the total number of square feet in this house? _____ How many fire extinguishers should this home have?_____ Think of a good location for each fire extinguisher; then draw one fire extinguisher symbol for each extinguisher needed on the floor plan above.

3. A house should also contain at least two carbon monoxide (CO) detectors. *(Carbon monoxide is a colorless, odorless, and deadly gas that can sometimes escape from faulty furnaces.)* Draw two CO detectors on the floor plan using this symbol ⊿⊿⊿ .

4. Two exit routes should be made for every room in the house in case of a fire. Using two different colored pencils or crayons, draw two escape routes from each bedroom and the kitchen to the outside of the house.

5. So that every family member can be accounted for, your family should have a specific place to meet outside of the house after escaping a fire. Where would be a good place for your family to meet after escaping a fire?

APPLE MONTH

Apple Month is observed every year during the month of October. Celebrate the occasion with the following activities and reproducibles.

You Are The Apple Of My Eye

Create an appealing Apple Month bulletin board while teaching a figurative language skill—metaphor. Explain to students that a *metaphor* is a figure of speech in which two dissimilar things are compared without the use of *like* or *as*. One item being compared is spoken of as if it *were* the dissimilar item. Brainstorm familiar metaphors with students, such as "She's a bear in the morning!" or "My cat is a heating pad for my feet." Next have each student create a positive metaphor about a friend, a classmate, a teacher, or a family member. Have him cut out an apple from construction paper and write his metaphor on it. Display the metaphors on a bulletin board titled "You Are The Apple Of My Eye."

"Sense-ational" Apples

Get your class into a "sense-sational" apple mood with the following activity. In advance, position several samples of apple-pie potpourri around the classroom. As the students inhale the sweet, spicy smell of the potpourri, ask them to list adjectives that describe the aroma. Then have students respond to questions, such as, "Are all pleasant smells something to eat?" and, "Is everyone's opinion the same?" Next provide each student with an apple and one copy of page 14. Have the student follow the directions on the sheet to examine how each of the five senses is stimulated by the apple.

An Orchard Of Apple Art

Explore the art of still life with an intense look at apples. Provide each student with an apple, one sheet of drawing paper, and colored pencils, pastels, watercolors, crayons, and/or markers. Divide students into pairs or groups of four. Explain to each pair or group that it will be arranging a still-life display using the apples. Students may peel, cut, stack, or group the apples in any way to create an appealing display. Give students time to draw the apple displays. Frame the drawings with red and green construction paper; then have each student state the art medium he used and explain why he felt this was the best medium for creating his still life. Mount the drawings on a bulletin board titled "An Apple Orchard Gallery."

"Sense-ational" Apples

There's more to the apple than its wonderful aroma! Closely examine your apple as you respond to each section below.

Sight

Look at your apple. Notice the shape, size, and color. Write as many words and phrases as you can think of that describe the appearance of your apple.

_____

_____

_____

Touch

Feel your apple. Notice the surface, temperature, shape, and weight. List as many words and phrases as you can that describe how the apple feels to you.

_____

_____

_____

Smell

Smell your apple. Cut or bite into the apple. Does it smell different on the inside? Make a list of words and phrases that describe how your apple smells.

_____

_____

_____

Sound

Slowly bite into your apple. Listen carefully to the sounds that are made. List words that describe the sounds made when you bit into your apple.

_____

_____

_____

Taste

Now, eat your apple. Is it sweet, tart, or bland? Does the meat of the apple taste the same as the skin? Write words and phrases that describe the taste of your apple.

_____

_____

_____

Bonus Box: Use at least two words or phrases from each section above to write a poem about an apple.

"Apple-icious" Math

Bite right into these grade-A apple math challenges! Solve each problem; then write your answer in the space provided.

1

North Carolina produces about 7,619,000 bushels of apples each year. California produces about twice as many. About how many bushels does California produce each year?

2

Washington State produces 110,317,000 bushels of apples each year. If Michigan grows 87,857,000 fewer bushels, how many bushels does Michigan grow?

3

One bushel of apples weighs 42 pounds. New York State raises about 22,000,000 bushels a year. What is the weight of New York's yearly crop?

1. _____

2. _____

3. _____

4

An apple usually has 10 seeds. How many seeds could be found in the 54,600,000 apples grown each year in Japan?

5

A young apple tree starts to bear fruit in its fifth year. In what year will trees planted in 1999 start to bear fruit?

6

Apple trees can produce fruit for as long as 100 years. If a tree produced a total of 879,137 apples over its lifetime, what would its yearly average be?

4. _____

5. _____

6. _____

7

It takes about 8 apples to make a pie. If a baker has 7 Granny Smith, 4 Empire, 6 McIntosh, 1 Cortland, and 17 Gala apples, how many pies can he bake?

8

Apples are Canada's most important fruit crop. A total of 30,000,000 bushels are grown each year: 4,373,000 in Quebec; 9,115,000 in Ontario; and 9,626,000 in British Columbia. The rest are grown in Nova Scotia and New Brunswick. How many bushels are grown in these two provinces?

9

A woman in Vermont thought it would be nice to surround her property with apple trees. She planted 1 tree every 15 feet all around her yard. She used 747 trees. What is the perimeter of her property?

7. _____

8. _____

9. _____

The FBI And The Apple Pie

Congratulations! You have just been named the head investigator of The Applesauce Double Cross! Here are the facts:

- Eight apples were bought to make applesauce.
- The apples have disappeared.
- An apple pie was found cooling in the kitchen.
- Several witnesses have come forward.
- You have recorded the clues on the notecards below.

Now it's time to put the clues in "apple-pie order" and discover what has happened. List the clues in the correct order on the lines below and solve the case of The Applesauce Double Cross.

Mildred G. Delicious was caught wearing hot mitts and taking something out of the oven.

The oven was on when Jonathan Gala had his coffee break.

I discovered a great birthday surprise.

An undercover agent claimed that Corey Cortland cored the apples.

Max McIntosh saw Agent Gertrude "Granny" Smith peeling the apples.

Winston "The Worm" Spry was said to have sliced the apples into a shallow pan.

I entered the room as everyone yelled, "Surprise!"

Anna Appleby was seen washing the apples and placing them in a bowl.

A distinct cinnamon smell was in the air when Mr. Hector Hedmin, the director, left the kitchen.

Ms. Orchard's floury fingerprints were found on a rolling pin.

1. _____

2. _____

3. _____

4. _____

5. _____

6. _____

7. _____

8. _____

9. _____

10. _____

The (Not So) Big Apple

New York City is known as the Big Apple because of its prestige as a cultural and entertainment center. New York City is the home of the nation's leading theater district, many large museums and art galleries, a great number of outstanding orchestras, the opera, and many famous dance companies.

Directions: Your challenge is to prove why *your* hometown is also worthy of the nickname the Big Apple. Complete the web below by writing details (reasons) and examples in each circle to support your opinion. Then use the information to write a persuasive paragraph on a separate sheet of paper, stating your opinion and backing it up with your supporting details.

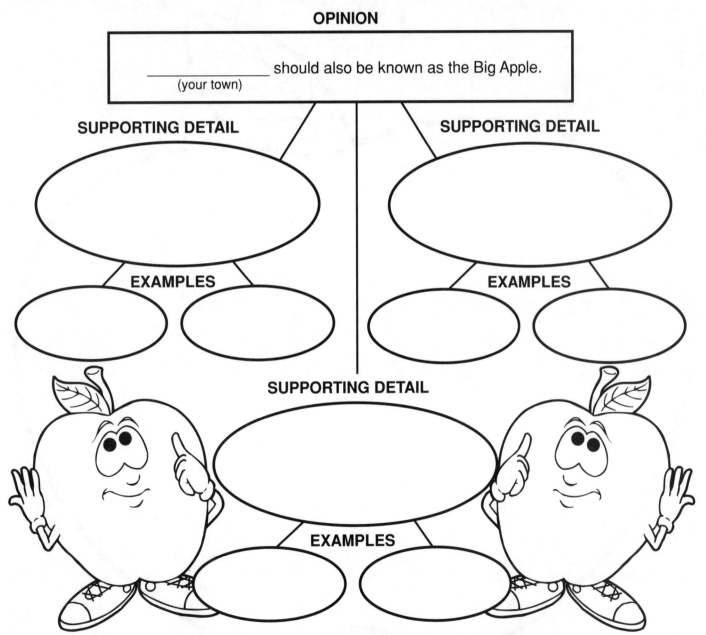

OPINION

_____ should also be known as the Big Apple.
(your town)

SUPPORTING DETAIL

SUPPORTING DETAIL

EXAMPLES

EXAMPLES

SUPPORTING DETAIL

EXAMPLES

Note To The Teacher: Prior to completing this page, explain to students that in persuasive writing, a writer presents her opinion on a topic. The writer then provides reasons and examples to support her opinion in an effort to get the reader to agree with her point. Explain to students that it is helpful for a writer to organize her thoughts prior to writing and that clustering ideas in a web related to the topic is one method of organizing ideas.

The Great Apple Substitution

Mrs. Appledumpling is your substitute teacher for the day. Substituting is what she loves most! She especially loves to substitute apples for objects and characters found in stories. Two of her favorite stories to tell are "Snow White And The Seven Apples" and the story of Pinocchio and how his nose grew every time he ate an apple. Now she wants you to create some new apple-substitution stories to add to her collection!

Directions: Choose a familiar folktale, fairy tale, or legend. Rewrite it by substituting apples for objects or characters in the story. Trace the apple pattern below onto several sheets of lined paper. Write your story on the lined apple sheets. Then use the pattern to design a cover. Include the title, your name, and an illustration on your cover. Staple the cover to the front of your story pages.

Note To The Teacher: Duplicate one copy of this page for each student. Before writing, help students brainstorm a list of common folktales, fairy tales, and legends.

Leif Ericson Day

Leif Ericson Day (October 9) honors the Icelandic explorer who is believed to have been one of the first Europeans to set foot on North America. Ericson may have reached the North Atlantic coast, naming it Vinland, nearly 1,000 years ago. A Viking-type settlement discovered in Newfoundland matched Ericson's description of Vinland.

Viking Research

When you think of the Vikings, is your first thought of fierce warriors who terrorized many seaside towns in Europe? Is that an accurate picture of this Scandinavian group? Have your students research to find out. Divide your students into pairs. Assign each pair one of the following research topics: economic activities, family life, religion, culture, food, clothing, housing, warfare, or shipbuilding. Have each group record its data on a 17" x 22" sheet of white construction paper. Schedule a time for each pair to present its findings; then compile all the posters into a big book about Vikings. Have a group of students illustrate a cover on a separate sheet of paper, and title the book "Vikings—Fact Or Fiction."

Viking "Prow-ess"

The prow (front end) of a Viking warship curved gracefully upward and ended with a wood carving of spirals, a dragon's head, or a snake's head. The carvings were embellished with glittering metal fittings.

Use the following activity to turn your students' desks into Viking ships! Have each student follow the directions below to create his own Viking ship figurehead. When each student has completed his figurehead, have him turn his desk into a Viking ship by taping his figurehead to the prow of his desk! *(If you do not have desks in your classroom, attach the figureheads to a bulletin board, creating a 3-D display.)*

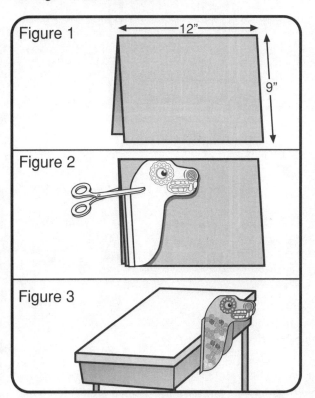

Figure 1

12"

9"

Figure 2

Figure 3

Materials For Each Student: one figurehead pattern from page 20, one 12" x 18" sheet of white construction paper, one paper clip, scissors, crayons or markers, tape
Directions:
1. Fold the sheet of construction paper in half (see Figure 1).
2. Place the figurehead pattern along the folded edge of the sheet of construction paper as shown in Figure 2. Use a paper clip to hold the pattern in place.
3. Carefully cut along the outline of the pattern.
4. Decorate the resulting two-sided figurehead with crayons or markers.
5. Fold each tab outward; then tape each tab to the front of your desk (see Figure 3).

Pattern

Use with "Viking 'Prow-ess' " on page 19.

(Place top of head along folded edge.)

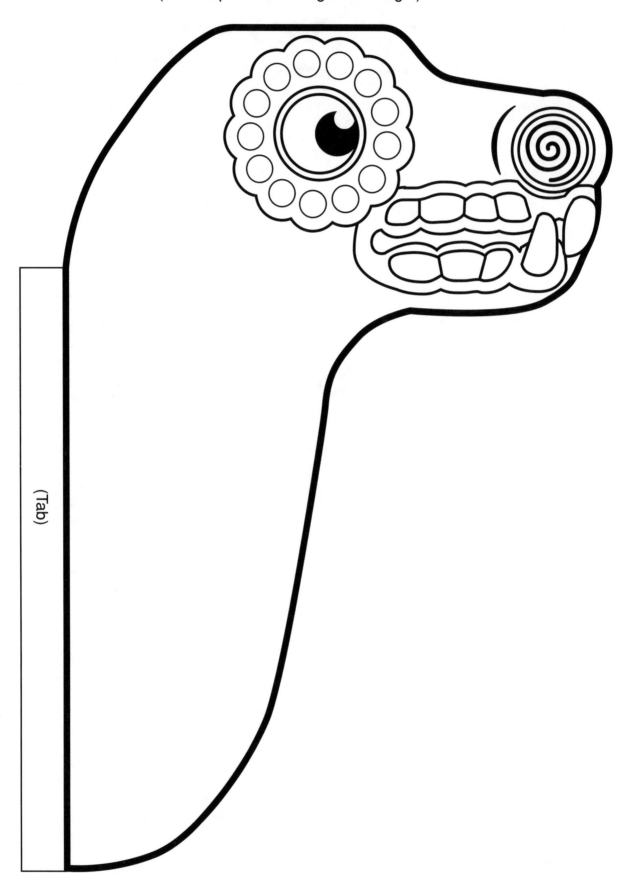

(Tab)

Journal Of An Explorer

Directions: What would it feel like to be the first person to see and record the sights of a new land? Research the plants, wildlife, and natural physical features of Newfoundland. Then, on the blanks below, write a brief description of what a member of Leif Ericson's crew might have written in a journal when reaching the North Atlantic coast of Newfoundland. Add illustrations in the boxes provided.

Plants: _____

_____

_____

_____

_____

_____

_____

_____

_____

Wildlife: _____

_____

_____

_____

_____

_____

_____

Physical Features: _____

_____

_____

_____

_____

_____

_____

_____

_____

Overall Impressions: _____

_____

_____

_____

_____

_____

What Did It Take To Be A Viking?

Part 1: On the left side of the chart below, list five personality traits necessary to be a member of Leif Ericson's crew of explorers. On the right side of the chart, briefly explain the importance of each trait.

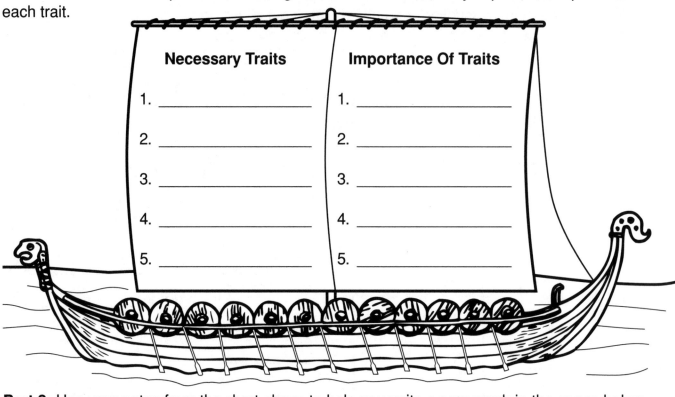

Necessary Traits

1. _____
2. _____
3. _____
4. _____
5. _____

Importance Of Traits

1. _____
2. _____
3. _____
4. _____
5. _____

Part 2: Use your notes from the chart above to help you write a paragraph in the space below explaining what kind of person would most likely have been a member of Ericson's crew. Be sure to begin your paragraph with a topic sentence.

_____

_____

_____

_____

_____

_____

_____

_____

_____

_____

Bonus Box: On the back of this sheet, write a paragraph explaining whether or not you have the traits needed to be a member of Ericson's crew.

Land Ho!

The Vikings sailed from Scandinavia in three main directions from the 700s to the 1000s. The Danes raided Germany, France, England, and Spain to the south. The Swedes explored eastern Europe. The Norwegians sailed to North America. Answer the questions and complete the activities below to retrace the Norwegians' exploration route.

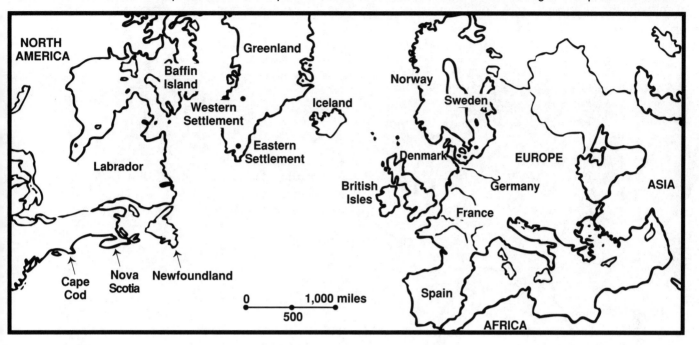

Directions:

1. Leif Ericson's father, Eric the Red, was born in Norway. When he was about ten years old, he moved with his father to Iceland. Use a brown colored pencil to trace a path from the southwestern shore of Norway to the western edge of Iceland. Use the map scale to estimate to the nearest 500 miles the distance of their journey. _____ miles

2. Leif Ericson was born in Iceland. When he was about five years old, his family sailed to Greenland and founded a settlement on the southwest coast (called the Eastern Settlement). Draw a green line on the map to show this journey. Make sure to "sail" around the southern tip of Greenland. Estimate the mileage of this journey. _____miles

3. The Vikings sailed farther up the western coast of Greenland and founded another settlement (called the Western Settlement). Continue the green line from the Eastern Settlement to the Western Settlement. It is believed that this is where Leif Ericson began his explorations.

4. Around the year 1000, Leif Ericson and a crew of 35 men went in search of land sighted by another sailor on a previous journey. Ericson sailed west from the Western Settlement, then veered south at Baffin Island and landed at northern Labrador. He continued sailing south to the southern end of Labrador. Continuing south, Ericson finally went ashore, naming this site Vinland, or Wineland, because of the many grapes he found growing. Most historians believe that Vinland is present-day Newfoundland—a Canadian province. Mark Ericson's route from Greenland to Vinland in red. Estimate the mileage of this journey. _____miles

5. Christopher Columbus discovered San Salvador Island in the Caribbean Sea in 1492. If Leif Ericson did in fact discover Newfoundland, Canada, in approximately 1000, how many years before Columbus had the Vikings discovered the New World? _____years

Name _____

Viking Vs. Viking

Was the Minnesota Vikings' football team named after the Scandinavian warriors of the past? The Vikings below are wearing different types of protective equipment. Compare the two. Then complete the diagram below by listing the similarities and differences in the types of protective gear.

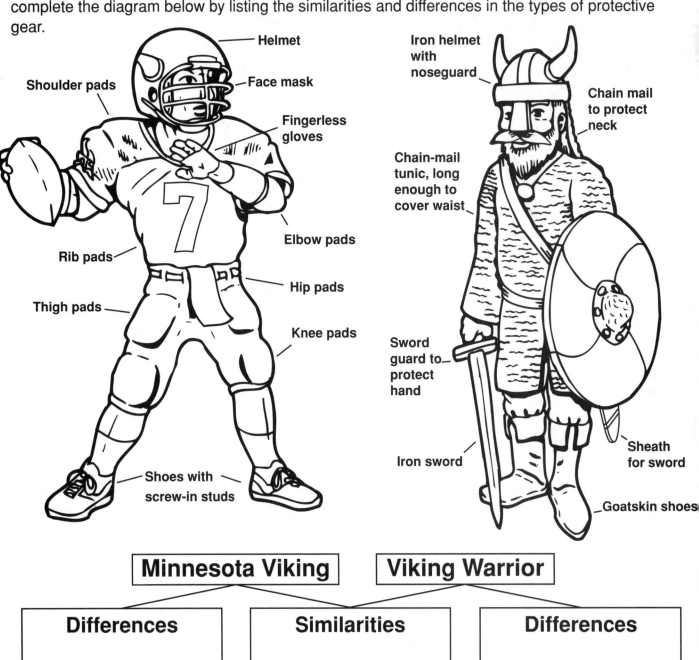

Helmet

Face mask

Fingerless gloves

Shoulder pads

Elbow pads

Rib pads

Hip pads

Thigh pads

Knee pads

Shoes with screw-in studs

Iron helmet with noseguard

Chain mail to protect neck

Chain-mail tunic, long enough to cover waist

Sword guard to protect hand

Iron sword

Sheath for sword

Goatskin shoes

Minnesota Viking		Viking Warrior
Differences	**Similarities**	**Differences**

International Letter Writing Week

International Letter Writing Week was established by the 14th Universal Postal Congress in 1957. The aim was to contribute to world peace by encouraging cultural exchanges through correspondence among the people of the world.

Commemorative Creations

Each year special commemorative stamps are issued in honor of International Letter Writing Week. Ask students, parents, or colleagues who may have stamp collections to share some of the International Letter Writing Week stamps from previous years. Also check with your local post office to see if the current commemorative stamp or any of the previous stamps are available to purchase. After viewing past and present International Letter Writing Week stamps, have each student design his own stamp for the occasion. Give each student one copy of page 27 and a supply of crayons or markers. Have each student share his stamp with the rest of the class and explain what his stamp design represents. Post the completed stamps on a bulletin board titled "Commemorative Creations."

Personalized Letterhead

Nothing will impress a pen pal more than to read a letter written on personalized letterhead. Have students create their own personalized stationery with the following activity. Duplicate five to ten copies of page 28 for each student. Then instruct the student to write his first and last name and his address in the center of the two-inch margin at the top of each sheet. Finally, in the area around his name in the margin, have the student include illustrations and/or clip art that reflects his hobbies or various interests. Encourage your students to use their letterhead whenever writing to a friend or pen pal.

International Pen Pals

Students love writing to pen pals and receiving mail from pen pals. Contact one of the organizations at the right to obtain a foreign pen pal for each student in your classroom. Have each student write to his new pen pal and describe the area in which he lives, including the climate, geographical features, and any points of interest. Have the student ask his pen pal to write back detailing the same information for the area in which he lives. Post a large world map on a bulletin board. Each time a student receives a letter from his pen pal, post a map pin or miniature flag to mark the country in which the pen pal lives. Also post around the map any pictures or illustrations that the pen pals may include in their letters.

World Cultural Foundation
P.O. Box 2480
North Bend, WA 98045-2480
e-mail: travelr@wcf.org
Web site: www.wcf.org
(valid as of 9/98)

International Penfriends
P.O. Box 1016
East Camberwell Vic 3126
Australia
e-mail: penpals@ozemail.com.au
Web site: www.ozemail.com.au/~penpals
(valid as of 9/98)

_____
(student's name)

Pen Pal Folder

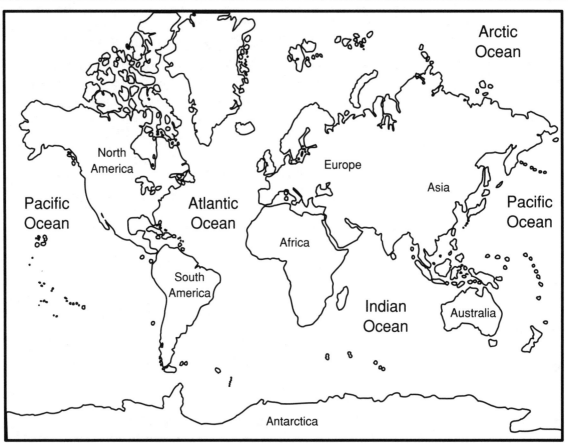

Note To The Teacher: Have each student staple a copy of this page to the outside of a file folder. Direct the student to store letters she receives from her international pen pals inside her folder. Instruct the student to make a red dot on the world map above to mark the approximate location from which each letter originated.

International Letter Writing
Commemorative Stamp Design
Created by

_____
(student's name)

Note To The Teacher: Use with "Commemorative Creations" on page 25.

Note To The Teacher: Use with "Personalized Letterhead" on page 25.

NATIONAL DESSERT MONTH

National Dessert Month is observed each year during the month of October to celebrate the sweet world of desserts. National Dessert Day is held annually on the second Thursday of October.

How Sweet It Is!

Sweeten your students' vocabulary with the following activity during National Dessert Month. Brainstorm with students a list of dessert words, such as cake, pie, candy, etc. Then explain to students that there is more to desserts than just cakes and pies. Distribute one copy of page 30 to each student. Read aloud to your students the dessert words on the page. Direct each student to use a dictionary or other resource book to find the definition and word origin for each dessert vocabulary word. Then have the student record the information on the appropriate recipe card.

A Collection Of Confections

Conclude your study of National Dessert Month by completing a Classroom Confectionery Cookbook! Have each student contribute a favorite family dessert recipe to the class cookbook. Allow parents to send in samples of the recipes if desired. Ask several parent volunteers to key in each recipe on the classroom computer. Compile the recipes into a book; then make a copy for each student. Encourage the student to illustrate his copy of the cookbook. Finally, have each student take his confectionery cookbook home to share with his family.

Desserts Around The World

Help your students enhance their geography skills while learning about desserts from around the world with the following activity. At the beginning of October, divide the class into groups of four students. Provide one copy of page 31, a blank sheet of paper, and a file folder for each group. Instruct each group to staple its copy of page 31 onto the left side of the folder and a blank sheet of paper onto the right side of the folder. Throughout the month, challenge each group to find recipes from around the world by reading through cookbooks, researching at the library, and interviewing friends and family members. Direct each group to keep a record on the blank sheet of paper that shows the name of each dessert, the country of origin of the dessert, and the chief ingredient. Then have the group color in the country that each dessert originated from on its map. Also have the group keep a copy of each recipe in its folder. Explain to groups that they will earn one point for each recipe recorded, with only one recipe per country allowed. At the end of the month, have groups share and compare their recipes; then award a prize to the group who acquires the most points.

How Sweet It Is!

Sweeten your vocabulary by using a dictionary or other resource book to find the definition for each dessert word below. Record the definition in the space provided on each recipe card.

1. Custard
_____
_____
_____
_____
_____

2. Trifle
_____
_____
_____
_____
_____

3. Meringue
_____
_____
_____
_____
_____

4. Soufflé
_____
_____
_____
_____
_____

5. Torte
_____
_____
_____
_____
_____

6. Tart
_____
_____
_____
_____
_____

7. Strudel
_____
_____
_____
_____
_____

8. Baklava
_____
_____
_____
_____
_____

9. Savarin
_____
_____
_____
_____
_____

10. Cruller
_____
_____
_____
_____
_____

11. Sorbet
_____
_____
_____
_____
_____

12. Compote
_____
_____
_____
_____
_____

Bonus Box: On the back of this page, create a word-search puzzle using the dessert vocabulary words above. Add any other dessert words you can think of to your puzzle. Then exchange puzzles with a classmate for some sweet vocabulary fun!

©1999 The Education Center, Inc. • *October Monthly Reproducibles* • Grades 4–5 • TEC962 • Key p. 63

Note To The Teacher: Use with "How Sweet It Is!" on page 29. Provide each student with one copy of this page, a dictionary, and other appropriate resource books.

National Dessert Month: map skills

Desserts Around The World

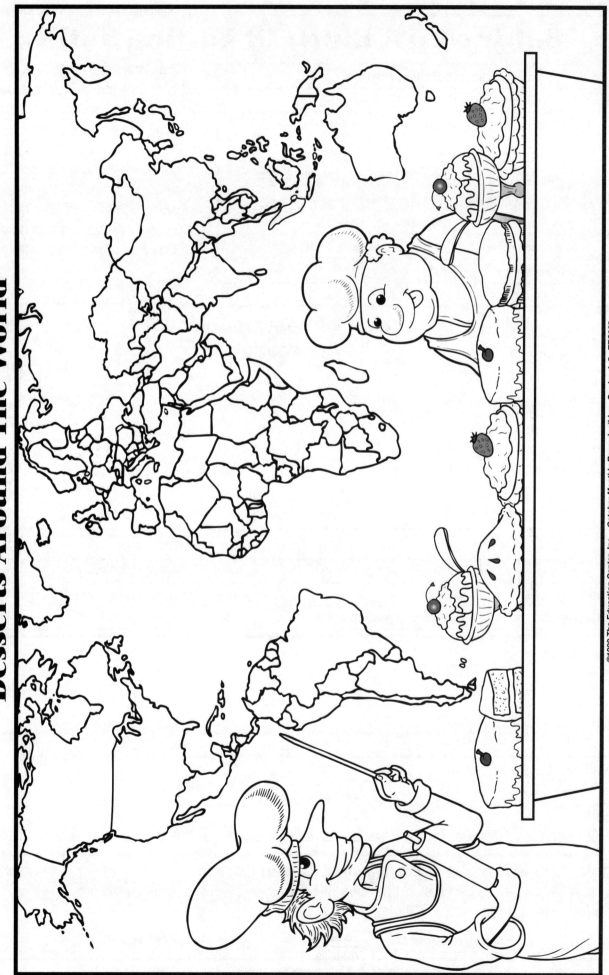

©1999 The Education Center, Inc. • *October Monthly Reproducibles* • Grades 4–5 • TEC962

Note To The Teacher: Use with "Desserts Around The World" on page 29. Provide each group with one copy of this page, a blank sheet of paper, and a file folder.

Baking Up A Batch Of Editing Skills

Common Editing Marks

symbol	meaning	example
⬭	Check spelling.	The ice (creme) melted.
⊙	Add a period.	She licked the lollipop⊙
⋏,	Add a comma.	The cake needed eggs̖butter, and milk.
⌄'	Add an apostrophe.	The chefs hat is tall.
☰	Make capital.	the baker sliced the pie.
/	Make lowercase.	An ice C̸ream cone is tasty.
⌒	Close gap.	I ate the ca͝ke.

Chef Wannabe's goal is to be accepted at the School Of Dessert Science. His application has been rejected several times due to mistakes in punctuation, capitalization, and spelling. Help Chef Wannabe achieve his goal by proofreading his application below. Then use the editing symbols in the box to correct his mistakes.

School Of Dessert Science Application

Date: October 14 1999 _____

Name: Chef I Wannabe _____

Address: 3515 Doughnut circle _____
        Street

    Hershey   Pa   20202
     City   State   Zip

Education

	Name Of School	Location Of School
High School	Trifle High	Sweet Home oregon
College	University Of Sweetwater Station	Wyoming

References:

1.   Chef Boy R. Dee   232 Spaghetti boulevard
              Name   Address

2.   Mr D. Hines   101 Cakeleaf Lane
              Name   Address

Previous Experience:

1.   I was the pie sli cer at miss Sweettree's bakery _____

2.   last year i delivered frozen deserts two the local grocery stores. _____

Why do you want to attend the School Of Dessert Science?

Ive always wanted to bee a world famous dessert chef. I want to lern how to prepare delicious pies puddings, and Cakes.

Signature: *Chef Wannabe* _____ **Date:** *October 14, 1999* _____

COLUMBUS DAY

Columbus Day—the second Monday in October—celebrates the sighting of San Salvador Island in the Caribbean Sea on October 12, 1492, by Christopher Columbus. Known as the person who "discovered" America, Columbus was searching for a shorter route to the Indies. He sailed west across the Atlantic Ocean in a fleet of three ships: the *Niña,* the *Pinta,* and the *Santa María.* For his efforts, Columbus was awarded the title Admiral Of The Ocean Sea.

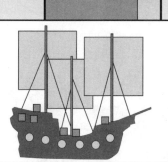

Getting Shipshape

Celebrate Columbus Day with this attractive geometric bulletin board. Have each student cut a ship's basic shape from brown construction paper. Next direct her to cut familiar geometric shapes—such as squares, circles, triangles, etc.—from different-colored construction paper. Then have her glue the resulting cutouts to her basic shape. Launch these seaworthy vessels on a wavy blue background titled "In Shape To Sail With Columbus."

Namesake Contest

Challenge your students to discover Columbus's influence on geographic names with this interesting investigation. Divide your students into groups; then give each group an atlas and a map of the Western Hemisphere. Have the groups search these resources, listing as many places whose names are similar to Columbus's (for example, Columbia; British Columbia; Columbus, Ohio; and Colombo, Brazil) as they can find. After a reasonable amount of time, have each group share its list. As each group shares, track the number of names shared and add their findings to chart paper to create a class compilation of names. After all groups have shared, recognize the group who found the most names. If desired, allow students to add more names to this list during free time.

Clerihews For Columbus

Inspire the young poets in your classroom to compose a special kind of verse about Columbus. Tell students that a *clerihew* is a four-line rhyming poem about a famous person. Help students brainstorm a list of words that rhyme with Columbus, such as *us, bus, fuss,* and *trust.* Next share some brief biographical information about Columbus. Then challenge each student to write a clerihew about Columbus, using at least one fact from the information you shared. Not only will your students practice a different type of poetry, but they'll learn fascinating facts about Columbus, too!

Ships Ahoy!

King Ferdinand and Queen Isabella of Spain provided the ships for Christopher Columbus's historic voyages. Launch your own fleet of ten ships by following the directions on this page!

Directions: Notice that the anchor for each sentence below contains a word beginning or ending with "ship." Read each sentence, and study its underlined phrase carefully. Then find a word in the Captain's Log that means about the same as the underlined phrase. Fill in the blank with the part of the word that completes each spelling.

King Ferdinand and Queen Isabella of Spain agreed to <u>pay for</u> the ships and supplies that Columbus needed on his voyage.

1. _____ship

Columbus probably made sure that everything on board the *Niña,* the *Pinta,* and the *Santa María* was <u>in good condition</u> before he set sail.

2. ship_____

<u>Being a part of</u> the crew was an adventure for many young men and boys.

3. _____ship

The crew members had to <u>join together and agree</u> to handle the sails and ropes and pump out water that washed aboard.

4. _____ship

During the voyage across the Atlantic Ocean, the explorers <u>suffered from hunger, thirst, confinement, and fear.</u>

5. _____ship

As more and more time passed with no sign of land, the crew began to question Columbus's <u>ability to make decisions.</u>

6. _____ship

When Columbus finally landed, he claimed the land for Spain. Then he and his men <u>held a religious ceremony.</u>

7. _____ship

At first the explorers and the Arawaks, the native people, <u>got along fine by treating each other with respect and kindness.</u>

8. _____ship

Some crew members felt that Columbus favored his brother because <u>he was related to him.</u>

9. _____ship

Columbus brought <u>goods, such as gold trinkets and exotic plants and animals</u> back to Spain.

10. ship_____

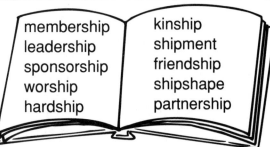

membership
leadership
sponsorship
worship
hardship

kinship
shipment
friendship
shipshape
partnership

Bonus Box: Think of another word that begins or ends with "ship." On the back of this paper, write and illustrate a sentence that shows its meaning.

©1999 The Education Center, Inc. · *October Monthly Reproducibles* · Grades 4–5 · TEC962 · Key p. 63

Porthole Peeks

Pretend you are a member of Columbus's crew, peering from a porthole as you cross the Atlantic Ocean on one of his historic voyages. Inside each porthole below, draw a scene showing what you "see" or imagine. Then color the illustrations.

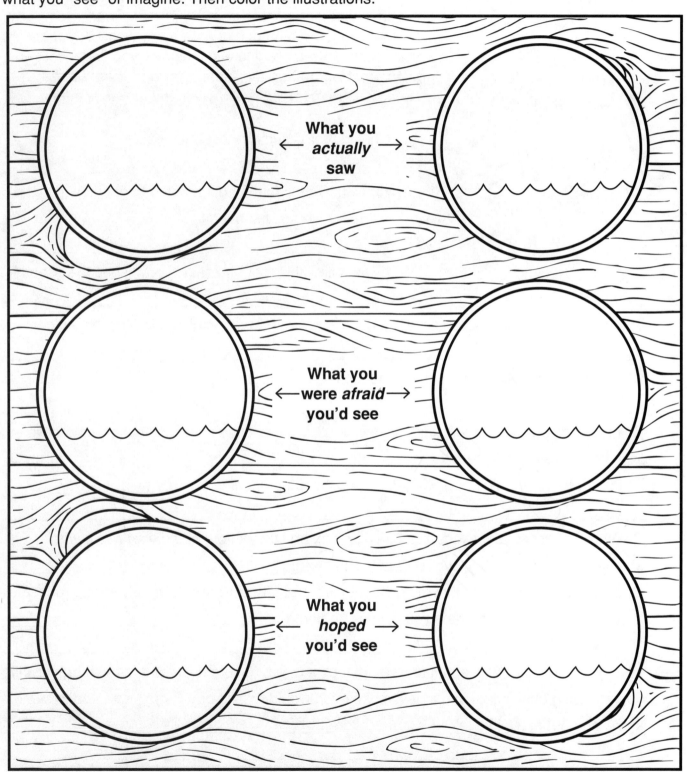

What you ← *actually* → saw

What you ← were *afraid* → you'd see

What you ← *hoped* → you'd see

Bonus Box: Draw a larger version of one of your scenes above on a paper plate so that it looks like a scene viewed from a real porthole. Then on the back of this sheet, describe how this paper-plate scene can help explain *trompe l'oeil,* an art expression that means "to fool the eye."

Note To The Teacher: Give each student one copy of this sheet, crayons or colored pencils, and a white paper plate.

Watt Dew Ewe No About Columbus?
(What Do You Know About Columbus?)

Directions: *Homophones* are words that sound the same but have different meanings and spellings. Read each sentence below to find one or more homophones that are used incorrectly. Underline each mistake you find. Then write the correct word(s) on the line(s) provided. *Hint: Each sentence's number tells you how many mistakes it has.*

1. Christopher Columbus loved the see.

   _____

2. He would stand in the bough of the boat and watch the waves brake against the ship.

   _____

3. "If we follow this root," he said, "we will bee their soon."

   _____

4. The cabin buoy tolled the captain that sum of the crew were planning a mutiny that knight.

   _____

5. Columbus guest that his sun did knot no those plans were maid.

   _____

6. Columbus faced his men and said, "Chews mutiny oar choose to weight four one more weak. Buy then, we will land or turn back." _____

7. Awl threw that chili knight, the wind blue, and the cent of fear was in the heir.

   _____

8. Columbus might have preyed, "Hour sale is torn, and the bottom of the boat has a whole. Maybe this feet was to big four us. Show us the weigh." _____

9. Of coarse, spending a lot of thyme on a ship that sighs wood ware down any strong man, but it wood really bee hard four the young boys on bored. _____

   _____

10. Write when the crew was about to give up, they saw a bird sore overhead, a fresh branch with flours floating on the tied, and a peace of carved would drifting buy. Every I strained to see a knew land. What a tail to tell their grandchildren! _____

   _____

Bonus Box: On the back of this sheet, write another sentence about Columbus. Use one of the following homophone pairs in your sentence: here/hear, led/lead, heard/herd, new/knew, knows/nose, stare/stair, ate/eight, pause/paws.

©1999 The Education Center, Inc. • *October Monthly Reproducibles* • Grades 4–5 • TEC962 • Key p. 63

36 **Note To The Teacher:** Duplicate one copy of this sheet for each student.

Columbus's Place In Time

Directions: Cut out the illustrations below. Study each illustration, and read its caption carefully. Then arrange the illustrations in the order that these events happened.

Columbus died on May 20, 1506. Later, his remains were moved to Santo Domingo.

Columbus returned to Spain on March 15, 1493, but he dreamed of returning to the beautiful island he had found in the New World.

In 1500, during Columbus's third trip to the New World, he was arrested and chained, bringing his career as the governor of an island to an end.

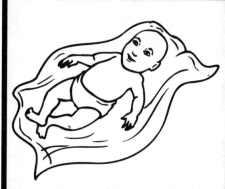

Christopher Columbus was born in 1451 in Genoa, Italy. He became interested in navigation when he was 14 years old.

On August 3, 1492, the *Niña,* the *Pinta,* and the *Santa María* set out from the port of Palos, Spain.

Columbus's second voyage focused on establishing permanent Spanish control of the islands.

Columbus's long search for financial support led him to the king and queen of Spain.

On Columbus's first voyage, he explored several Caribbean islands.

Columbus hoped to gain honor and wealth by sailing west to reach the Spice Islands in the East.

©1999 The Education Center, Inc. • *October Monthly Reproducibles* • Grades 4–5 • TEC962 • Key p. 63

Note To The Teacher: Give each student scissors and one copy of this sheet. Direct the student to staple the illustrations together in the correct order to form a booklet. Then have him make a cover for his booklet. *Or* instruct the student to glue the illustrations in correct order on construction paper to form a timeline comic strip and add a title frame at the beginning.

Welcome To The "W W W" Show!
(Who? What? Where?)

Play along with the cast of this wild, wacky, and wonderful quiz show that delights in asking the popular questions "Who Am I?", "What Am I?", and "Where Am I?" Just write an answer in each category box below. You're bound to come out a winner!

WHO? (Who Am I?)	WHAT? (What Am I?)	WHERE? (Where Am I?)
① I am Columbus's brother who ran a mapmaking shop. Who: _____	② I am the title that was granted to Columbus by King Ferdinand and Queen Isabella. What: _____	③ I am the city where Columbus was born and spent most of his boyhood. Where: _____
④ I am the woman Columbus married in 1479. Who: _____	⑤ We are the items that Europeans wanted to get from the East. What: _____	⑥ I am the country that sponsored Columbus on his voyages. Where: _____
⑦ I am the son of Columbus who sailed with him on his fourth voyage to the New World. Who: _____	⑧ I am the date on which Columbus first reached land in the Western Hemisphere. What: _____	⑨ I am the group of islands where Columbus got fresh supplies for his first voyage across the Atlantic Ocean. Where: _____
⑩ I am the king of Spain who helped pay for Columbus's adventures. Who: _____	⑪ I am one of the ships provided for Columbus's first voyage. I am not the *Niña* or the *Santa María*. What: _____	⑫ I am the place where Columbus thought he had landed. Where: _____
⑬ I am a member of the group of natives Columbus found on San Salvador. Who: _____	⑭ I am the name Columbus gave to the natives he found in the New World. What: _____	⑮ I am the island where Columbus first landed in the New World. Where: _____

Bonus Box: Use the back of this sheet to write three more questions and answers like those above, one for each category.

WORLD SERIES

In 1903 the leaders of the National and American leagues met to determine the champion of baseball in the very first World Series. The series has been held every year since then, except for 1904 and 1994.

Personal Baseball Cards

Baseball cards contain vital information and statistics about the players. Share a variety of baseball cards with your students. What important information would your students share with the world if they could be featured on trading cards? To find out, have each student create a trading card about himself. Create a template by cutting around an actual trading card on a piece of tagboard. Use this template to cut out enough cards for the entire class. Instruct each student to draw a self-portrait or glue a photo of himself on one side of his card. On the other side, have the student list actual accomplishments or goals he hopes to achieve in the future (example: first woman on Mars, founder of Computers 'R Us, holder of record for "Star Trek" trivia, etc.). Have each student temporarily trade his card with a classmate to learn even more about each other. Then have students return cards back to the original owners. Encourage each student to use his trading card as an inspirational bookmark, one that will always remind him that he's a star player!

First Woman On Mars!
☆ ☆ Founder Of ☆
☆ Computers 'R Us ☆
Star Trek Trivia Champion

Stadium Statistics

Make statistics a grand slam in your classroom by using the sports page. Before this activity, gather the sports pages from your local newspaper for several days. Then pass out one full page or clipping to each student. Using examples from your math text, direct students to write story problems that can be solved by using the information in the newspaper box scores and summaries. Have your students exchange problems with each other and solve them. Then have each student discuss his strategies for solving each problem.

1. How many hits did Lopez make compared to Lemke?
2. Compare the scores of Irving and Glavine. Who scored...

Baseball's History

Make baseball a history lesson with this idea that's a home run! Many exciting events occurred throughout baseball's history. Have students research its background using encyclopedias, almanacs, or library books. Using your history text, demonstrate the elements of a timeline. Then have your students create a timeline on the history of baseball. To extend this activity, create a living timeline. Divide your students into pairs, then assign each pair a date to act out. Bring history to life by having the pairs act out their dates in order! Events may include the following:

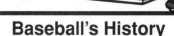

1846	The first game is played, using Alexander Cartwright's rules.
1903	The first World Series is played.
1944	Joe Nuxhall becomes the youngest major-league player in history at 15 years, 10 months old.
1951	Topps begins printing baseball cards.
1970	The aluminum bat is introduced.
1981	Players go on strike for 50 days.
1989	An earthquake strikes California during the World Series.
1998	Mark McGwire breaks Roger Maris's record by hitting more than 61 home runs.

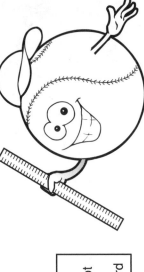

Does Baseball Measure Up?

Use the baseball diamond and information box to help you complete the problems below.

Information Box

- perimeter—total distance around a closed figure
- area—length x width in square units

- 12 inches = 1 foot
- 3 feet = 1 yard
- 36 inches = 1 yard

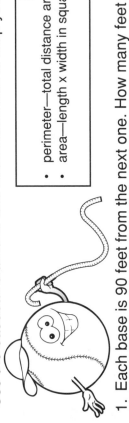

1. Each base is 90 feet from the next one. How many feet must a batter run if he hits a double? Triple? _____ Home run? _____

2. How many inches is it from the center of the pitcher's mound to home plate? _____

3. How many yards is it from the center of the pitcher's mound to home plate? (Round to the nearest yard.) _____

4. How many square feet make up the area of the infield? _____

5. List three different closed figures that can be identified in the diagram. Trace their outlines in blue. _____

6. If the right-handed batter's box is 6 feet by 4 feet, what is its perimeter? _____ Area? _____

7. Approximately where on the playing field would a batter be if he ran 225 feet after hitting the ball? _____

8. How many yards would a ball travel if a player bunted it straight to the pitcher? (Round to the nearest yard.) _____

9. How many feet would a baseball travel if a slugger cracked it 50 yards into the outfield? _____

10. How many inches would the baseball from question 9 travel if hit the same distance? _____

Diagram labels: outfield, second base, first base, third base, infield, pitcher, home plate, 90 feet, 90 feet, 60 feet, 6 inches

Play With Words

Each word below has two meanings. The meaning related to baseball is listed on the left. The non-baseball meaning is listed on the right. Read each word. Write the number of its baseball definition in the baseball. Then write the letter of its non-baseball definition in the baseball. The first one is done for you.

1. A play in which the batter is out, but succeeds in moving a teammate along on the bases

pitch, 4, E

A. To go faster than a walk

2. Originally, the infield, but now refers to the entire field

diamond

B. To give up or lose something

3. The score made by an offensive player who advances all the way around the bases to home

fly

C. A refusal to work by a group of workers

4. A ball delivered to the batter

sacrifice

D. A great success

5. A one-base hit

single

E. To set aside or discard by throwing

6. To handle a batted or thrown ball; also the area on which the game is played

hit

F. A precious stone known for its hardness and brilliance

7. A smooth, rounded stick, not more than 42 inches long

bat

G. A flying mammal that feeds at night

8. A batted ball that goes high in the air

strike

H. An area of cleared land used for pasture or crops

9. A pitch that passes through a recognized zone or is swung at by the batter and missed

run

I. A winged insect

10. A batted ball on which the batter reaches base

field

J. Not married

Bonus Box: Write a baseball and non-baseball definition for these words: bunting, choke, bench, batter, and battery.

Fractured "Yogi-isms"

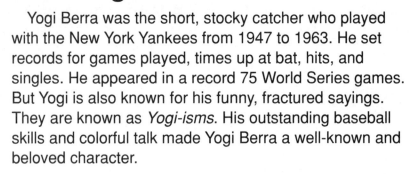

Yogi Berra was the short, stocky catcher who played with the New York Yankees from 1947 to 1963. He set records for games played, times up at bat, hits, and singles. He appeared in a record 75 World Series games. But Yogi is also known for his funny, fractured sayings. They are known as *Yogi-isms*. His outstanding baseball skills and colorful talk made Yogi Berra a well-known and beloved character.

Directions: Below are five actual statements made by Yogi Berra. Read each quote carefully and try to determine its meaning. Then, inside each bat, rewrite the saying so that it makes more sense to you.

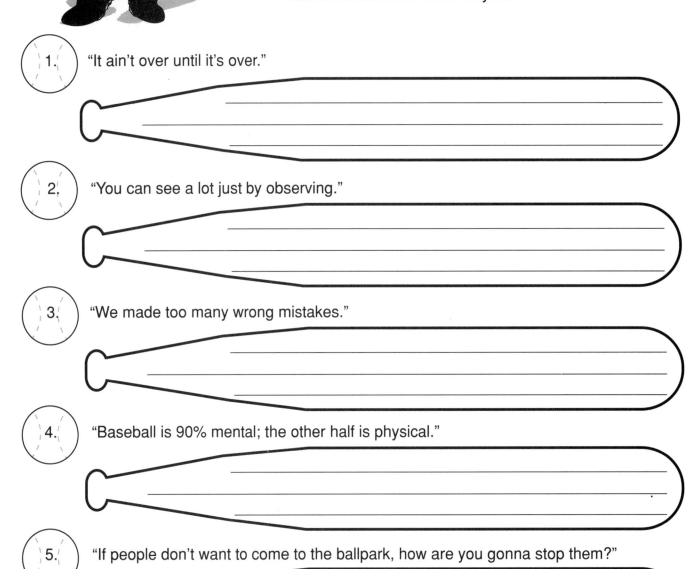

1. "It ain't over until it's over."

2. "You can see a lot just by observing."

3. "We made too many wrong mistakes."

4. "Baseball is 90% mental; the other half is physical."

5. "If people don't want to come to the ballpark, how are you gonna stop them?"

NATIONAL CLOCK MONTH

October is National Clock Month. Since prehistoric times, people have been interested in knowing the time of day. Sundials—the oldest known instruments for telling time—and hourglasses were not accurate means of telling time. The first reliable mechanical clocks were constructed during the 12th and 13th centuries. With the introduction of the pendulum in the 17th century, clocks greatly improved.

Types Of Timepieces

Invite your students to have the time of their lives investigating the different types of timekeeping devices. Divide students into groups of four. Ask each group to brainstorm as many different kinds of timepieces as possible, ranging from early methods to modern ones. Next have each group share its list with the class. As each group shares, record on chart paper the names of the different devices. Divide the devices into two categories: historic timepieces (sandglass or hourglass, water clock, sundial, candle clock, etc.) and modern timepieces (cuckoo clock, grandfather clock, alarm clock, wristwatch, pocket watch, etc.). Then give each group three minutes to divide the modern timekeepers into the two types below. Allow each group to share its groupings. Then reward the winning group(s) with ten minutes of free time sometime during the day!

• mechanical clocks—*clocks (usually dial clocks) that must be wound at different intervals*
• electric clocks—*clocks (usually digital clocks) that run on batteries or by current from an electrical outlet*

Counting The Hours

Help students understand the need for a standard means of world timekeeping. Tell students that over time sailors came to realize the need for a reliable clock in order to accurately navigate the seas and conduct commerce. Show students a map of the world's 24 time zones. Explain how these time zones—each 15 degrees of longitude wide—begin at Greenwich, England. Explain, too, that for each zone west of Greenwich, the time goes back one hour, and for each zone east of Greenwich, it moves ahead one hour. Next explain that in 1884 the International Date Line, an imaginary line at 180 degrees longitude, was added to maps to help world travelers know when one day changed to the next.

Using the current time of day, help students determine what time and day it is in New York City and several other cities around the world, such as London, Amsterdam, Hong Kong, and Tokyo. Next have each student pretend that he's planning a trip to another part of the world. Direct him to determine the current time and day in that place. Then have him write a paragraph telling why it would or would not be appropriate for him to contact someone in that place at the current time to make trip arrangements.

As The Pendulum Swings

Christian Huygens, a Dutch astronomer, invented the first pendulum clock in 1657. A *pendulum* is a rod with a weight, called a *bob,* at the end. The time it takes for the pendulum to swing back and forth one time is called a *period.*

Make your own version of a pendulum by following the steps below. Then use your pendulum to help you record data in the charts and answer the questions.

Materials: two same-sized metal washers, 30-inch length of string, tape, desk or table, clock with a second hand

Steps:
1. Tie one washer to one end of the string.
2. Tape the other end of the string to the edge of your desk.
3. Measure the distance between the tape and the knot. Record this length in the chart below.
4. Hold the washer so that the string is taut, perpendicular to the edge of the desk, and parallel to the floor.
5. Let the washer go so that it swings back and forth.
6. Repeat steps 4 and 5, recording the number of times the bob swings back and forth in one minute.
7. Shorten the string's length between the tape and the knot. Record this length in the chart.
8. Repeat step 6.
9. Repeat the entire activity using the same string lengths and two washers instead of one. Record the data for this trial in the chart.

	One Bob	Two Bobs
String Length	Number Of Swings Per Minute	Number Of Swings Per Minute

1. Did shortening the string affect the number of swings per minute? If so, how? _____

_____

2. Did adding another weight affect the number of swings per minute? If so, how? _____

_____

> **Bonus Box:** Based on your data above, how would using an even *longer* string affect the number of swings per minute? Adding a third washer?

Note To The Teacher: Pair students for this activity so that one student can watch the clock while the other works with the pendulum. Have students switch roles for step 9.

As The Clock Ticks

The workers at Clockworks Incorporated work hard each day. Solve the problems below to learn more about each employee's working hours.

1. Allen begins assembling dials at 8:15 A.M. If he stops for two 15-minute breaks, takes an hour for lunch, and leaves work at 4 P.M., how long has he worked? _____

2. Elaine's job is testing the chimes. After arriving at 9 A.M., she works steadily until noon. After an hour for lunch, she works until 4:45 P.M. Does Elaine work longer than Allen? _____ If so, how much longer? _____

3. Bob's job is testing the alarms on alarm clocks. If he's worked for 4 1/2 hours by noon, what time does he start work? _____

4. Sue works part-time putting glass covers on clock faces. How many hours does she work each week if she works Monday, Wednesday, and Friday mornings from 8:30 until 11:30, and Tuesday and Thursday afternoons from 1:30 until 4:30? _____

5. Stan's job is putting the weights in grandfather clocks. If he works eight hours, starting at 7:45 A.M. and taking one 15-minute break and an hour for lunch, what time does he leave work? _____

6. Pam hangs the pendulums in grandfather clocks beginning at 7:45 A.M. If she works 2 1/2 hours before taking a break, what time is her break? _____

7. Hank puts the batteries in battery-powered clocks. If he works 4 hours 15 minutes more after his lunch ends at 12:45, what time is it when he goes home? _____

8. Michelle tests the springs in spring-driven clocks. What time does she arrive at work if she leaves at 5 P.M. after an eight-hour day? _____

9. Andy works in the stockroom from 9 A.M. until 11:45 A.M. each day, and on the loading docks from 1 P.M. until 3:30. Where does he spend more of his time? _____

10. Amy puts the electronic chips in clock mechanisms. What time is her lunch break if she takes it exactly 2 hours 45 minutes after her 9:45 A.M. morning break? _____

11. Brad checks the quality of the cuckoo clocks. If he takes a break 3 1/2 hours after he arrives at 7:15 A.M. and again 1 hour 45 minutes before he leaves at 4:30, what time are his breaks? _____ and _____

12. Doug works three afternoons each week oiling the clocks' gear mechanisms. If he works three hours per day and leaves at 6:45 P.M., what time does he start work? _____

> **Bonus Box:** Who works more hours per week, Sue or Andy?

©1999 The Education Center, Inc. • *October Monthly Reproducibles* • Grades 4–5 • TEC962 • Key p. 64

Beat The Clock!
A Game For Two Players

Race against the clock to see who can
be the first player to reach 100!

The catch? If a player rolls doubles after the first roll, he has to subtract two points from his running total!

Materials: pair of dice, pencil, clock with a second hand

Directions:
1. Write your name in the chart below.
2. Ask your partner to time you for a period of two minutes.
3. At "Go," roll the dice, and write the number rolled in the space marked "1st roll" on the chart.
4. Roll again, and write this number in the space marked "2nd roll."
5. Find the sum of these two numbers, and write it in the space marked "Sum."
6. Continue rolling the dice and recording the numbers, keeping a running total of the sum until time is up. Use the back of this page if you run out of space.
7. Switch roles, having your partner roll the dice while you keep the time.
8. When time is up, circle the sum that's closer to 100 without going over to determine the winner of this round.
9. Play additional rounds as time permits.

	Round 1		Round 2		Round 3	
	Player #1:	Player #2:	Player #1:	Player #2:	Player #1:	Player #2:
1st roll						
2nd roll						
sum						
3rd roll						
sum						
4th roll						
sum						
5th roll						
sum						
6th roll						
sum						
7th roll						
sum						
8th roll						
sum						
9th roll						
sum						
10th roll						
sum						

©1999 The Education Center, Inc. · *October Monthly Reproducibles* · Grades 4–5 · TEC962

46   **Note To The Teacher:** Duplicate one copy of this page for each pair of students.

How Long Does It Take?

How long does it take to tie your shoelace or hum "The Star-Spangled Banner"? Just follow the directions below to find out!

Directions:
1. Read the four tasks below. Estimate how many seconds you'd need to do each task. Write your estimates in the chart below.
2. Do each task. Have a teammate time you and record your actual time in the chart.
3. Mark the column that shows how your estimate compares with your actual time for each task.

Task #1: Tie your shoelace.
Materials: a shoe with untied laces, a clock with a second hand

---

Task #2: Hum one verse of "The Star-Spangled Banner" or "Hickory Dickory Dock."
Materials: a clock with a second hand

Task #3: Count backward from 50 to zero.
Materials: a clock with a second hand

Task #4: Write the name of the current month on paper 12 times.
Materials: paper, pencil, a clock with a second hand

50, 49, 48,...

Time In Seconds				
Task	Estimate	Actual	Close	Not Close
Tie shoelace				
Hum song				
Count backward				
Write month				

Bonus Box: Add the task of cleaning out your desk to the chart above. Do this task, following the same procedure as before. Then enjoy your clean desk!

Note To The Teacher: Pair students, making sure that one student in each pair is wearing a laced shoe and that each pair has access to a wall clock (or watch) with a second hand. Make one copy of this sheet for each student.

It's Writing Time!

Bring a story about a really unique timepiece to life. The possibilities for settings and plots can be endless! To get started, just complete each step below in order. Choose one or more items from each category to help you write your tale. Feel free to add your own ideas, too. And remember to indent each time you start a new paragraph. It's always the right time to write!

Steps:
1. Choose one timepiece.
2. Write one or more sentences to introduce your timepiece.
3. Write a few sentences describing your timepiece's appearance.
4. Write one or more sentences describing the setting of your story.
5. Write several sentences describing the story's problem.
6. Write a few sentences describing how the problem is solved.
7. End the story with a good concluding sentence.

Timepieces
- grandfather clock
- alarm clock
- mantel clock
- cuckoo clock
- wall clock
- digital clock
- pocket watch
- wristwatch
- waterproof watch

Settings
- in a cozy kitchen
- in a small living room
- in a modern office building
- on a store shelf
- on a speeding truck
- on a slow-moving freight train
- in a dingy warehouse
- in a damp basement
- inside a wooden crate
- near a pier

Names
- Crazy Crompton
- Hannah Hopper
- Waldo Worthington
- Poovy Fitzsimmons
- Sparky Spudrucker
- Big Ben
- Officer Bob
- Mr. Nichols
- Ruby Riffle

Problems
- the missing clock
- the clock that ran fast
- the clock that ran slow
- the clock that ran backward
- the alarm clock that wouldn't ring
- the lost watch
- the broken watch

Appearance
- hand-carved
- steely gray
- dull and tarnished
- rough and uneven
- old and scratched
- smooth and shiny
- broken
- chained
- rusty
- gold
- silver
- covered with dust

Bonus Box: Illustrate your favorite part of the story on a sheet of drawing paper. In a space on the drawing, write a sentence describing your scene.

©1999 The Education Center, Inc. • *October Monthly Reproducibles* • Grades 4–5 • TEC962

THE WHITE HOUSE

On October 13, 1792, the cornerstone for the White House was laid. In 1800, John Adams and his family became the first presidential family to occupy the White House. This historic building has three stories, over 100 rooms, and is the oldest building in Washington, DC.

Soup's On! Come And Get It!

Have you ever wondered what's being served for dinner in the White House? Astound your students by sharing some of the following favorite foods of presidents:

Abraham Lincoln—oysters served lots of different ways
Dwight D. Eisenhower—prune whip
John F. Kennedy—fettucini
George Bush—Tex-Mex chili and Chinese take-out food
Lyndon Johnson—corn pudding
Grover Cleveland—corned beef and cabbage
Richard Nixon—cottage cheese topped with ketchup

"Soup's on!"

Give each student one sheet of drawing paper and markers or crayons. Then have each student illustrate a picture of her favorite dish. Instruct the student to write a brief description of the dish at the bottom of the page. Post the completed drawings around the classroom for everyone to read and enjoy.

Four-Legged Friends Of The White House

Astound your students by telling them that when Theodore Roosevelt became president in 1901, he brought with him six children and lots of pets. The White House was alive with dogs, cats, squirrels, raccoons, rabbits, guinea pigs, a badger, a black bear, a rat, a parrot, and a green garter snake! Also tell your students that when Archie Roosevelt came down with the measles and had to remain in his room on the second floor, he was cheered up by a visit from Algonquin, the family's pet pony! How did he get there, you ask? Like anyone else—he rode the elevator!

Have each student write about their favorite pet or about a pet they hope to have one day. Instruct each student to write one paragraph describing the pet and one paragraph explaining why this pet is so special to his family. If the child is writing about a pet he hopes to have one day, have him explain why this particular pet would be so special to his family. Have each student share his writing with the rest of the class; then post the illustrations on a bulletin board titled "Precious Pets."

Name The Presidents

Make a game out of learning the names of the presidents in order with the following activity. Read aloud *Yo, Millard Fillmore! And All Those Other Presidents You Don't Know* by Will Cleveland and Mark Alvarez (The Millbrook Press, Inc.; 1997). This book uses humorous illustrations to tell a strange, connected story that helps students remember the order of the presidents. After reading the book, have each student develop his own wacky method of remembering the presidents in order. List the first five presidents on the board; then instruct each student to use the first letter of each president's name listed as the first letter in a word. Have the student write the words in order to create a wacky sentence. (See the example.)

Example: Washington, Adams, Jefferson, Madison, Monroe

What **a** **j**olly **m**olly **m**ess.

Continue the process with the next five presidents until each student has included all the presidents' names in several wacky sentences. Allow time for students to practice their wacky sentences; then see if any student can repeat all of his sentences, as well as name the presidents, in the correct order.

Fact-Finding Frame

Directions: John Adams and his family were the first presidential family to live in the White House. Learn more about the second president of the United States by researching the answers to the missing facts in the frame below. Write each answer in the appropriate space above or below each heading.

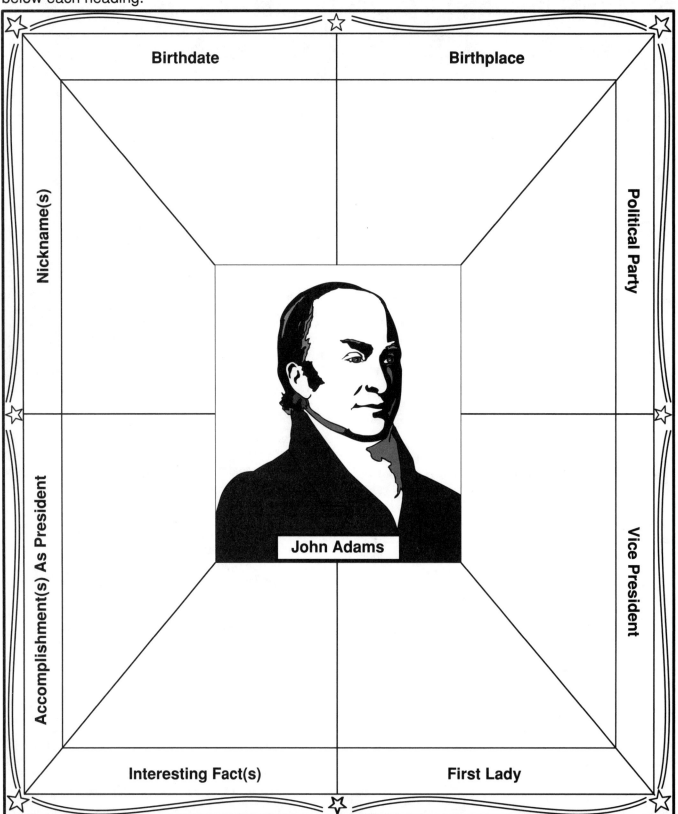

Birthdate

Birthplace

Nickname(s)

Political Party

Accomplishment(s) As President

John Adams

Vice President

Interesting Fact(s)

First Lady

©1999 The Education Center, Inc. • *October Monthly Reproducibles* • Grades 4–5 • TEC962 • Key p. 64

Famous First Ladies

Directions: The wife of the president—the first lady—has one of the most interesting positions in America. Even though she is not elected like the president, she can have a great deal of influence. Research to find out what each first lady below contributed to America during her husband's term in office. Record your findings on the blanks provided.

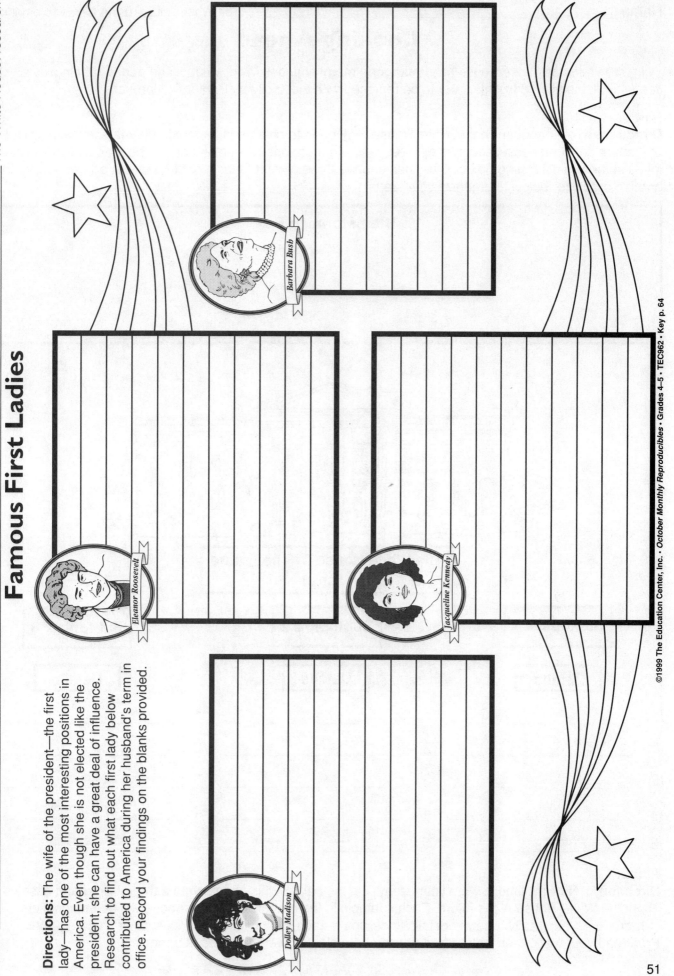

Barbara Bush

Eleanor Roosevelt

Jacqueline Kennedy

Dolley Madison

Looking Ahead

In 200 years the White House has undergone many changes. Andrew Jackson added running water. James Polk installed gaslights, later to be replaced with electricity by Benjamin Harrison.

Part 1:
Directions: Think about how the White House may need to change in the next 100 years. Brainstorm a list of modern conveniences, security measures, and other changes that may need to be made. Record your ideas in the Brainstorming Box below. Then choose three of your ideas to write about in an essay. Use the graphic organizer below to organize your ideas.

Brainstorming Box

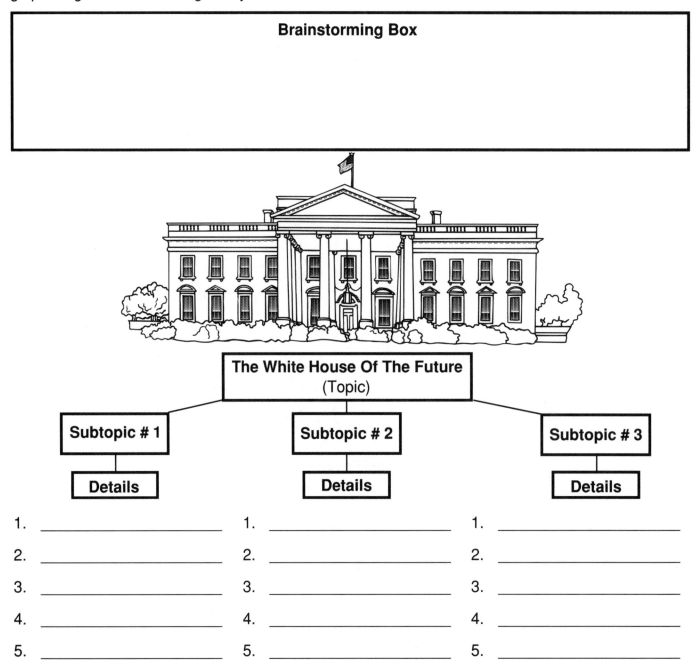

The White House Of The Future
(Topic)

Subtopic # 1	**Subtopic # 2**	**Subtopic # 3**
Details	**Details**	**Details**

1. _____	1. _____	1. _____
2. _____	2. _____	2. _____
3. _____	3. _____	3. _____
4. _____	4. _____	4. _____
5. _____	5. _____	5. _____

Part 2:
Directions: Now it's time to write your essay. On the back of this sheet, write a three-paragraph essay about the White House of the future. Each subtopic in the graphic organizer above will be the topic of a paragraph in your essay. Use the details underneath each subtopic in sentences for each paragraph. Proofread your work; then write a final version on a clean sheet of notebook paper.

National POPCORN POPPIN' Month

October has been deemed National Popcorn Poppin' Month by the Popcorn Institute. It is a time to celebrate popcorn as a wholesome, natural, and economical snack.

Popcorn Cake?

Celebrate National Popcorn Poppin' Month by making a popcorn cake with your class. Follow the directions below to create this delicious treat!

Ingredients:
3 tablespoons margarine
4 cups miniature marshmallows
1 cup small gumdrops
1 cup shelled peanuts
8 cups popped popcorn

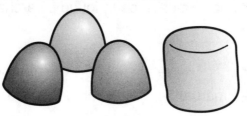

Directions:

In a saucepan, melt the margarine on low heat. Add marshmallows and heat until melted. In a bowl, mix the peanuts, gumdrops, and popcorn. Combine the marshmallow and popcorn mixtures and press firmly into a 9" x 13" greased pan. Makes twenty-four 2" x 2" servings.

Gee, this tastes stale!

The Lowdown On Popcorn

Did you know that archaeologists found popcorn that was 5,600 years old in a bat cave in New Mexico? Did you know that 1,000-year-old popcorn kernels were discovered in Peru and could still be popped? Share more cool facts about popcorn by reading aloud to your students Tomie dePaola's *The Popcorn Book* (Holiday House, Inc.; 1984). After reading the book, divide your students into pairs. Give each pair one sheet of poster board and crayons or markers. Instruct each pair to illustrate one interesting fact they learned about popcorn from dePaola's book. Serve popcorn to your class while each pair shares its poster with the rest of the class. Display the posters around the classroom during the month of October.

A Popcorn Wonderland

Just for fun, teach your students the following popcorn song, sung to the familiar tune of "Winter Wonderland." Then challenge your students to create more verses to the song.

Popcorn pops—are you listening?
Butter melts—see it glistening.
A sprinkle of salt,
We won't call a halt
Till we've eaten every kernel of corn.

At the gym, rink, or ballpark,
All day long till it gets dark.
We're at a good movie
Or just watching TV,
But we're eating great big bags of popcorn.

Repeat first verse.

Name _____

Pop Quiz

Directions: Choose the correct word from the word box below to complete each statement about popcorn.

```
                              Word Box
   • oldest    • peanuts   • oil       • popcorn    • Hemisphere
   • Peru      • inside    • oldest    • not        • Mexico
   • calories  • popcorn   • nutrients • television
   • pressure  • outer     • religious • Nebraska
```

1. __ __ __ __ __ __ __ is a light snack food that is very popular throughout the United States.

2. Popcorn is one of the __ __ __ __ __ __ forms of corn.

3. Thousand-year-old kernels of popcorn have been found by archaeologists in Utah and the South American country of __ __ __ __.

4. When eaten plain, popcorn is low in __ __ __ __ __ __ __ __.

5. Corn __ __ __ is used to make margarine, which can be melted and added to popcorn.

6. Some Native Americans used popcorn as part of __ __ __ __ __ __ __ __ __ ceremonies.

7. Illinois, Indiana, and __ __ __ __ __ __ __ __ are leading popcorn-producing states.

8. The United States grows almost all of the world's __ __ __ __ __ __ __ .

9. Popcorn kernels have hard __ __ __ __ __ shells and soft, moist, starchy centers.

10. When a kernel is heated, the moisture in it turns to steam and builds up __ __ __ __ __ __ __ __ inside the shell.

11. Sometimes popcorn is combined with __ __ __ __ __ __ __ and coated with caramel.

12. When a kernel reaches 400°F, it turns __ __ __ __ __ __ out.

13. A diet made up of only popcorn would lack important __ __ __ __ __ __ __ __ __ .

14. The leading corn-growing nations in the world are the United States, China, Brazil, and __ __ __ __ __ __ .

15. Popcorn is the __ __ __ __ __ __ snack food in the Americas.

16. Popcorn is __ __ __ eaten uncooked.

17. Popcorn is a favorite treat of Americans, often eaten in front of the __ __ __ __ __ __ __ __ __ __ or at the movies.

18. Popcorn was first grown in the Western __ __ __ __ __ __ __ __ __ __ .

Bonus Box: The first letter of each answer, written in order, will spell the name of a special event for popcorn lovers. Write each letter in the appropriate blank below to find out the name of this event.

__ __ __ __ __ __ __ __ __ __ __ __ __ __

Perfectly Popped Popcorn

Alliteration is the repeating of the beginning consonant sound in words, as in the sentence "**S**ally **s**ells **s**eashells by the **s**eashore." On the lines below, write a story about Paul—the perfectly popped popcorn kernel. Include as many appropriate words as possible that begin with the letter *p*. Make the story humorous and fun. Be prepared to read your story aloud to your classmates.

_____
(title)

National Popcorn Poppin' Month: word maze

The Popcorn "Maize"

Ever pop some popcorn and end up with only half the kernels popped? What happened? To find out and also learn how to keep this problem from occurring again, solve the maze below.

Directions:
1. Begin at START.
2. Use a pencil to trace from word to word to spell out the solution. Use every word in the message only once. The message is made up of more than one sentence.
3. Move up, down, left, right, and diagonally.
4. End at FINISH.

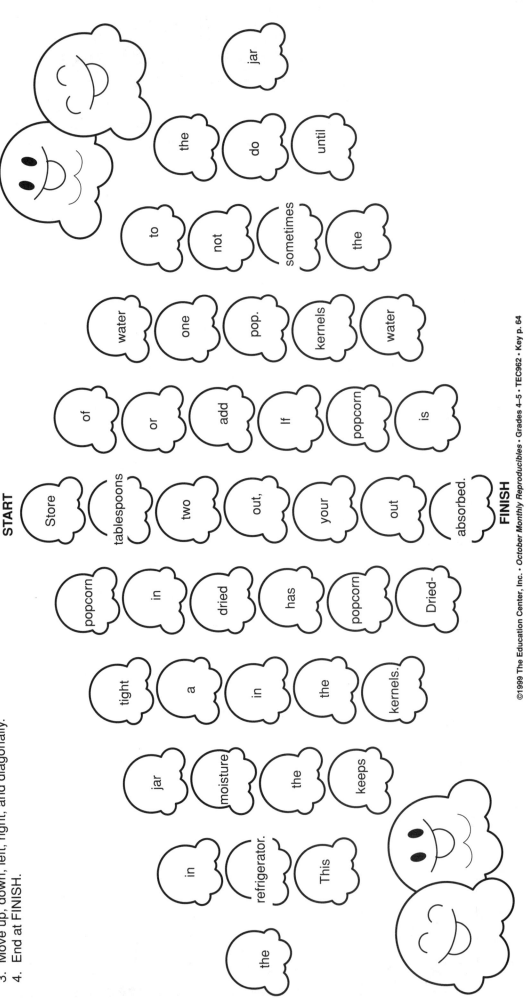

jar

the   do   until

to   not   sometimes   the

water   one   pop.   kernels   water

of   or   add   If   popcorn   is

START

Store   tablespoons   two   out,   your   out   absorbed.

FINISH

popcorn   in   dried   has   popcorn   Dried-

tight   a   in   the   kernels.

jar   moisture   the   keeps

in   refrigerator.   This

the

©1999 The Education Center, Inc. • *October Monthly Reproducibles* • Grades 4–5 • TEC962 • Key p. 64

HALLOWEEN

Halloween is celebrated each year on October 31. It originated from the ancient harvest festival *Samhain,* a time of the year when people believed that the spirits of the deceased roamed the earth. In the 1840s, Irish settlers brought to America their Halloween customs, which included bobbing for apples and lighting jack-o'-lanterns.

Counting To Halloween

Harness the excitement that brews among students before Halloween; then use it to review important basic concepts and skills. On a sheet of poster board, draw a large haunted house with 31 windows. Cut open each window to make a flap as shown. Number the outer side of the flaps from 1 to 31. Glue the haunted house to another sheet of poster board. (Do not glue the flaps down.) Write a math problem or review question in the space behind each flap. Beginning with number 1 and working toward number 31, open a flap each day in October and have students complete the problem or review question behind it.

Halloween How-Tos

Enhance expository-writing skills by challenging each child to write a how-to paragraph on one of the following topics: bobbing for apples, carving a jack-o'-lantern, trick-or-treating, face painting, or making candied or caramel apples. Provide each student with a sheet of orange construction paper. Direct the student to cut out a pumpkin from his paper; then glue his completed paragraph to the cutout. Post the completed work on a bulletin board titled "A Patch Of Halloween How-Tos." Connect the pumpkins with vines cut from green construction paper.

Pumpkin Vital Statistics

Get your students pumped up for estimation with the following activity. Gather a pumpkin, tape measure, kitchen scale, bathroom scale, carving knife, and large spoon. Have each student make a chart like the one shown. Show students the pumpkin; then have each child complete the "Estimate" column of her chart. Next have student volunteers find the actual count and measurements for categories 1–4 on the chart. Instruct each child to record these results on her chart. Have your class vote on how the pumpkin should be carved. Then carve the pumpkin and continue taking actual measurements and counting for categories 5–7 on the chart. Discuss how students' estimates compare to the actual measurements. Reward your hardworking estimators with their favorite Halloween treats!

Pumpkin Fact	Estimate	Actual	Difference
1. Number of outer rings			
2. Circumference (inches)			
3. Height			
4. Weight before carving			
5. Weight of seeds and pulp			
6. Weight after carving			
7. Number of seeds			

Halloween Hysteria

After weeks of careful planning, the kids of Haunted Hollow chose their Halloween costumes and were ready for a fun-filled night of trick-or-treating. Complete these fun logic puzzles to find out more about their night.

Directions: Use the clues below to match each costume to the child who wore it. Keep track of the information given by using the chart. Put a √ in each box that is true and an X in each box that is not true.

	ballerina	ghost	cheer-leader	scare-crow	magician	soccer player
Malorie						
Jimmy						
Hanna						
Christopher						
John						
Michael						

Clues:
1. The cheerleader is a girl.
2. Jimmy, Christopher, and Michael are not the magician.
3. Hanna was a ballerina last year, so she decided to be something different this year.
4. Christopher's mother used straw to make his costume.
5. Jimmy did not want to be a ghost because his friend was going to be one.

The kids of Haunted Hollow collected lots of candy during their trick-or-treating. Some of the children visited more houses than others visited, so they received more candy.

Directions: Use the following clues to number the children 1 to 6 in order from the child who visited the most houses to the child who visited the least houses.

Clues:
1. Jimmy went to more houses than Michael but less than Hanna.
2. John went to more houses than Jimmy but less than Hanna.
3. The only child to go to less houses than Malorie was Christopher.

Malorie _____
Jimmy _____
Hanna _____
Christopher _____
John _____
Michael _____

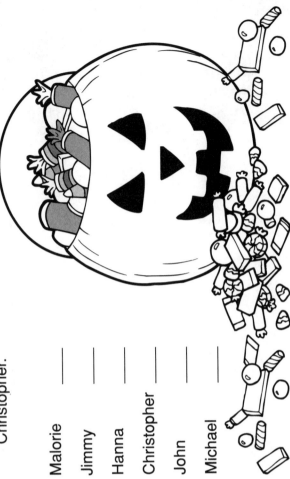

Graveyard Grammar

A *common noun* is a general name of a person, a place, a thing, or an idea and is not capitalized unless it is at the beginning of a sentence.

Examples: witch, pumpkin, graveyard

A *proper noun* is the specific name of a person, a place, a thing, or an idea and is always capitalized.

Examples: Dr. Frankenstein, Elm Street, M&M's®

Directions: Read the nouns on each tombstone below. Circle the proper noun in each. On the line provided, rewrite each proper noun and insert capital letters as needed. Then rearrange the underlined letters in the proper nouns to answer the riddle below.

1. pumpkin
   dr. jekyll
   ghoul
   _____

2. wanda witch
   haunted house
   cat
   _____

3. trick
   costume
   uma alien
   _____

4. werewolf
   mike monster
   cauldron
   _____

5. ben bit
   candied apple
   vampire
   _____

6. stephen king
   pillowcase
   jack-o'-lantern
   _____

7. candy corn
   count dracula
   alien
   _____

8. treats
   mr. hyde
   false teeth
   _____

9. goblin
   wolf
   terror trail
   _____

10. ghost
    alfred hitchcock
    bat
    _____

11. dracula drive
    moon
    spiderweb
    _____

12. mask
    francis fear
    candy bar
    _____

What song did DJ Dracula play at Gary and Greta Ghost's wedding?

"You Are So '_____,' _____ _____!"

"Di-Vine" Division: A Halloween Division Game

Directions For Two Players:

1. Put your game markers on the pumpkin marked "Start."

2. Player 1 rolls the die.

3. On scrap paper, Player 1 divides the number on the pumpkin he is on by the number on the die. Player 2 also works the problem to be sure the answer given by Player 1 is correct.

4. Player 1 then looks at the remainder of the division problem and moves ahead that many spaces. For example, if the remainder of the problem is 2, then Player 1 moves ahead 2 spaces.

5. If there is no remainder, Player 1 does not move ahead. Also, if the problem was worked incorrectly, the player does not move ahead.

6. Player 2 then repeats Steps 2–5. Players continue to take turns in the same manner.

7. The first player to reach "Finish" with the exact remainder needed wins. If a player does not have the exact remainder needed to reach "Finish," that player remains on that same space, and play continues.

Pumpkins (numbers shown): 31, 8, 47, 42, 53, 28, 9, 12, 29, 19, 17, 61, 33, 46, 37, START 43, 11, FINISH

Note To The Teacher: Divide your students into pairs. Supply each pair with one copy of this page, one die, scrap paper, pencils, and two different-colored plastic chips or paper squares to use as game markers.

Boning Up On Creative Writing

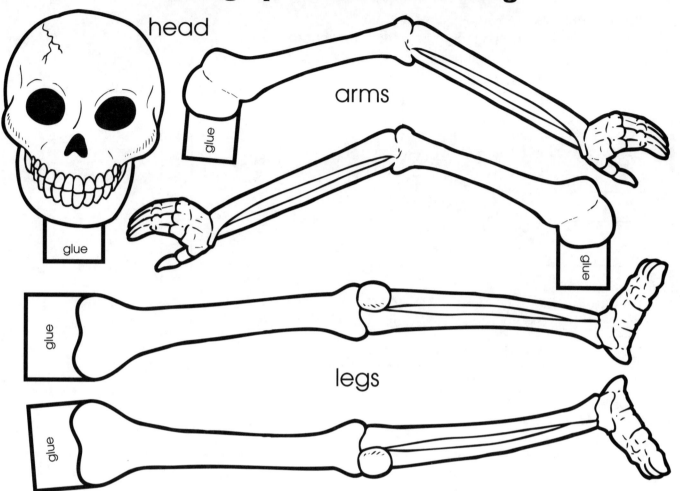

head

arms

glue

glue

glue

glue

legs

glue

glue

Example:

Directions:

1. Cut out the five, large skeleton parts above and set them aside for later.
2. Cut out the 20 word boxes below.
3. On a sheet of notebook paper, write a creative Halloween story using at least 10 of the 20 word bones in the story.
4. Each time you use a word, glue that word bone in the sentence on your notebook paper instead of writing the word.
5. When you have finished writing your story, glue the large skeleton parts to the notebook paper as shown.

ghost | cat | screamed | moaned | goblin | creaking | leaped | pumpkin | moon | scared | trembled | harvest | autumn | graveyard | laughed | costume | dark | sunset | shadow | candy

Note To The Teacher: Provide each student with one copy of this page, scissors, and glue.

Name _____

Trick-Or-Treat Trek

Frankie Stein, Wanda Witch, Drake Ula, and Sandy
Scream went trick-or-treating together in their neighborhood,
Haunted Hollow. Answer each question below to trace the
trick-or-treating route the children followed.

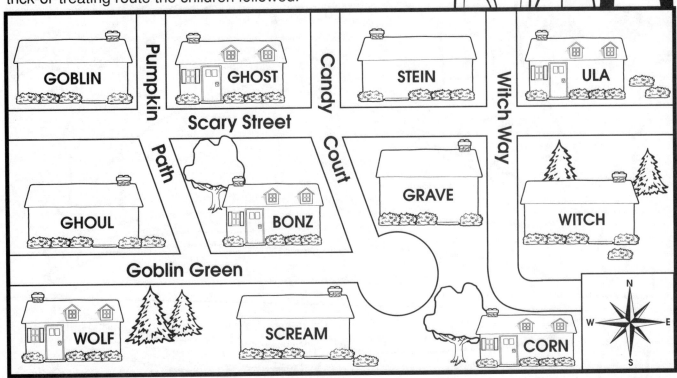

1. If the children began trick-or-treating at Wanda Witch's house and then went to Drake Ula's house, in which direction did they travel? _____

2. If they went to Frankie Stein's house after leaving Drake's house, in which direction did they travel? _____

3. After leaving the Stein house, the children went to the Grave house. In which direction did they travel to get there? _____

4. From the Grave house, they walked west. Which house did they reach next? _____

5. After leaving that house, the kids went to meet their friend Sandy Scream at her house so she could join them for trick-or-treating. In which direction did they travel? _____

6. From the Scream house, the kids went to the Wolf house. In which direction did they travel?
_____

7. The kids headed north after leaving the Wolf house. Which house did they reach next?
_____

8. The kids decided to go back to the Bonz house after visiting the Ghoul house. In which direction did they travel? _____

9. The kids headed directly north from the Bonz house. Which house did they reach next?
_____

10. In which direction did the children travel if they visited the Goblin house after leaving the Ghost house? _____

11. The Goblin house was the last house the kids visited on Halloween. In which direction did the kids travel on Scary Street to get back to their houses? _____

Answer Keys

Page 7
1. Charles M. Schulz
2. Robert Goddard
3. Eleanor Roosevelt
4. 1947
5. Nobel Peace Prize
6. the character from Sesame Street® who lives in the trash can
7. a dictionary
8. Russia
9. Jonas Salk

Page 8

	Embroidered apron	Lederhosen	Hiking boots	Dirndl skirt	Sauerkraut	Pumpernickel bread	Strudel	Frankfurter
Lester	✗	✓	✗	✗	✗	✗	✓	✗
Chester	✗	✗	✓	✗	✗	✗	✗	✓
Hester	✓	✗	✗	✗	✗	✓	✗	✗
Ester	✗	✗	✗	✓	✓	✗	✗	✗

Page 9
inclined plane: a simple machine with a sloping surface. An example of an inclined plane is a ramp, making it easier to slide a load upward than to lift it directly.

wedge: a special kind of inclined plane that moves. Wedges are used to separate objects or materials.

screw: an inclined plane wrapped around a cylinder or a cone. Its main purpose is to raise a load over the *threads* (the spiral part of the screw) by applying a small force.

pulley: a wheel around which a rope or chain is passed. A pulley is used to change the direction and point of application of a pulling force.

lever: a simple machine made up of a bar that turns, or pivots, around a fixed point. A lever helps lift weights with less effort.

wheel and axle: a simple machine made up of two wheels that turn, or pivot, around the same point.

Page 12

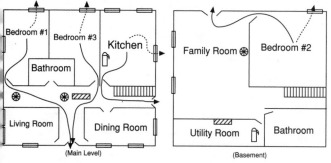

(Main Level)   (Basement)

Clues:
9. The main floor bathroom is 45 sq. ft. (9' x 5'). The basement bathroom is 84 sq. ft. (12' x 7').

Questions And Activities:
1. See floor plan above. Accept any approximate or reasonable locations for symbols.
2. This house has 1500 sq. ft. (each floor is 25' x 30'); 2–3 fire extinguishers would be needed. See floor plan above. Accept any approximate or reasonable locations for symbols.
3. See floor plan above. Accept any approximate or reasonable locations for symbols.
4. See floor plan above. Accept reasonable and logical escape routes.
5. Accept reasonable and logical family meeting locations.

Page 15
1. about 15,238,000
2. 22,460,000
3. 924,000,000
4. 546,000,000
5. 2004
6. 8791.37
7. 4
8. 6,886,000
9. 11,205 ft.

Page 16
Answers may vary slightly.
1. Anna Appleby was seen washing the apples and placing them in a bowl.
2. Max McIntosh saw Agent Gertrude "Granny" Smith peeling the apples.
3. An undercover agent claimed that Corey Cortland cored the apples.
4. Ms. Orchard's floury fingerprints were found on a rolling pin.
5. Winston "The Worm" Spry was said to have sliced the apples into a shallow pan.
6. The oven was on when Jonathan Gala had his coffee break.
7. A distinct cinnamon smell was in the air when Mr. Hector Hedmin, the director, left the kitchen.
8. Mildred G. Delicious was caught wearing hot mitts and taking something out of the oven.
9. You were seen entering the room as everyone yelled, "Surprise!"
10. You discovered a great birthday surprise.

Page 23

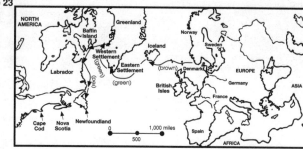

1. See map; about 1,000 miles.
2. See map; about 1,250 miles.
3. See map.
4. See map; about 1,250 miles.
5. About 492 years.

Page 24
Answers may vary. Possible answers listed below.

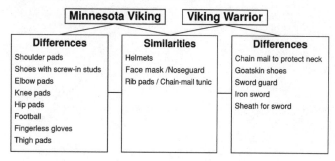

Minnesota Viking — **Viking Warrior**

Differences
Shoulder pads
Shoes with screw-in studs
Elbow pads
Knee pads
Hip pads
Football
Fingerless gloves
Thigh pads

Similarities
Helmets
Face mask /Noseguard
Rib pads / Chain-mail tunic

Differences
Chain mail to protect neck
Goatskin shoes
Sword guard
Iron sword
Sheath for sword

Page 30
1. **Custard**—a sweet, pudding-like mixture made of eggs and milk
2. **Trifle**—a dessert usually made of sponge cake; sherry, rum, or brandy; jam or jelly; fruit; custard; and whipped cream
3. **Meringue**—a dessert topping made of stiffly beaten egg whites and sugar
4. **Soufflé**—a baked dish made from a sauce, egg yolks, beaten egg whites, and flavoring
5. **Torte**—a cake made with many eggs, often grated nuts or dry bread crumbs, and covered with frosting
6. **Tart**—a small pie shell filled with jelly, custard, or fruit
7. **Strudel**—a pastry made of a thin sheet of dough rolled up with a filling and baked
8. **Baklava**—a dessert made of thin pastry, nuts, and honey
9. **Savarin**—a rich yeast cake baked in a ring mold and soaked in a rum or kirsch syrup
10. **Cruller**—a small sweet cake that is in the shape of a twist and deep-fried
11. **Sorbet**—fruit-flavored ice
12. **Compote**—fruit cooked in syrup

Page 32

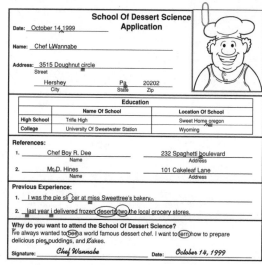

School Of Dessert Science Application

Date: October 14, 1999

Name: Chef L. Wannabe

Address: 3515 Doughnut circle
Street

Hershey   Pa   20202
City   State   Zip

Education

	Name Of School	Location Of School
High School	Trifle High	Sweet Home oregon
College	University Of Sweetwater Station	Wyoming

References:
1. Chef Boy R. Dee — 232 Spaghetti boulevard
   Name   Address
2. Mr. D. Hines — 101 Cakeleaf Lane
   Name   Address

Previous Experience:
1. I was the pie slicer at miss Sweettree's bakery.
2. last year i delivered frozen deserts two the local grocery stores.

Why do you want to attend the School Of Dessert Science?
I've always wanted to bee a world famous dessert chef. I want to lern how to prepare delicious pies, puddings, and cakes.

Signature: Chef Wannabe   Date: October 14, 1999

Page 34
1. sponsorship
2. shipshape
3. membership
4. partnership
5. hardship
6. leadership
7. worship
8. friendship
9. kinship
10. shipment

Bonus Box answer: Students' answers will vary. Suggested answers could include *shipman, shipmate, shipwreck, shipyard, penmanship,* and *workmanship.*

Answer Keys

Page 36
1. sea
2. bow, break
3. route, be, there
4. boy, told, some, night
5. guessed, son, not, know, made
6. Choose, or, wait, for, week, By
7. All, through, chilly, night, blew, scent, air
8. prayed, Our, sail, hole, feat, too, for, way
9. course, time, size, would, wear, would, be, for, board
10. Right, soar, flowers, tide, piece, wood, by, eye, new, tale

Page 37
1. Christopher Columbus was born in 1451 in Genoa, Italy. He became interested in navigation when he was 14 years old.
2. Columbus hoped to gain honor and wealth by sailing west to reach the Spice Islands in the East.
3. Columbus's long search for financial support led him to the king and queen of Spain.
4. On August 3, 1492, the *Niña*, the *Pinta*, and the *Santa María* set out from the port of Palos, Spain.
5. On Columbus's first voyage, he explored several Caribbean islands.
6. Columbus returned to Spain on March 15, 1493, but he dreamed of returning to the beautiful island he had found in the New World.
7. Columbus's second voyage focused on establishing permanent Spanish control of the islands.
8. In 1500, during Columbus's third trip to the New World, he was arrested and chained, bringing his career as the governor of an island to an end.
9. Columbus died on May 20, 1506. Later, his remains were moved to Santo Domingo.

Page 38
1. Bartholomew
2. Admiral of the Ocean Sea
3. Genoa (in Italy)
4. Felipa Perestrello Moniz
5. spices, gold, silk, gems
6. Spain
7. Ferdinand
8. October 12, 1492
9. Canary Islands
10. King Ferdinand
11. the *Pinta*
12. East Indies
13. Arawak (or Taíno)
14. Indians
15. San Salvador

Page 40
1. 180 feet, 270 feet, 360 feet
2. 726 inches
3. 20 yards
4. 8,100 square feet
5. (in any order) square, circle, pentagon
6. 20 feet, 24 square feet
7. Halfway between second and third bases
8. 20 yards
9. 150 feet
10. 1,800 inches

Page 41
1. sacrifice, B
2. diamond, F
3. run, A
4. pitch, E
5. single, J
6. field, H
7. bat, G
8. fly, I
9. strike, C
10. hit, D

Bonus Box answers:
Answers may vary. *(Baseball definition appears first.)*
bunting: hitting the ball with a push of the bat rather than a full swing; an infant's hooded sleeping bag
choke: to grip a bat several inches up from the end; to become obstructed in breathing or to lose one's composure and fail to perform effectively
bench: to remove a player from the starting lineup for playing poorly; a long seat for two or more persons
batter: the player whose turn it is to bat; a mixture used as a coating for food that is to be fried
battery: the pitcher and the catcher; a group of cannons

Page 42
Answers may vary. Suggested answers:
1. Don't give up. Keep working at it until the very end.
2. You can learn a lot by watching what is happening. Pay attention.
3. We made too many mistakes. Several things that we did were wrong.
4. Thinking about what you are doing is a very important part of baseball. But you must also be physically fit in order to play the game well.
5. You can't force people to make the choice that you want them to make.

Page 44
The time the pendulum takes to make one complete swing depends on the length of the rod, but each swing takes the same time. Shortening the string increases the number of swings per minute. Adding another weight (washer) does not cause the number of swings per minute for each length to change much at all.

Bonus Box answer: Based on the data, lengthening the string should cause the number of swings per minute to decrease. Adding a third weight (washer) should not cause the number of swings per minute at each length to change.

Page 45
1. 6 hours 15 minutes
2. Elaine works 6 hours 45 minutes, which is 30 minutes longer than Allen works.
3. 7:30 A.M.
4. (3 hours per day x 3 days) + (3 hours per day x 2 days) = 9 hours + 6 hours = 15 hours
5. 5 P.M.
6. 10:15 A.M.
7. 5 P.M.
8. 9 A.M.
9. stockroom
10. 12:30 P.M.
11. 10:45 A.M. and 2:45 P.M.
12. 3:45 P.M.

Bonus Box answer: Sue works 15 hours per week. Andy works longer at 26 hours 15 minutes per week.

Page 50
Birthdate: October 30, 1735
Birthplace: Braintree, MA
Political Party: Federalist
Vice President: Thomas Jefferson
First Lady: Abigail Adams
Interesting Fact(s): Accept any reasonable fact(s).
  Example: the only president to be the father of another president
Accomplishment(s) As President: Accept any reasonable answer(s).
  Example: founded the U.S. Navy
Nickname(s): "Old Sink or Swim"; "Duke of Braintree"

Page 51
Accept any reasonable responses. Some suggested responses are listed below.
Dolley Madison—Dolley Madison was one of the most successful first ladies. She was known for treating everyone she met with dignity.
Eleanor Roosevelt—Eleanor Roosevelt was known for her support of troops overseas during World War II and for her work to bring attention to the plight of victims of poverty, prejudice, and war. She was one of the first first ladies to give speeches and present her own ideas publicly.
Jacqueline Kennedy—Jacqueline Kennedy was known for her interest in the arts. She brought many cultural events to the White House. She also stressed the importance of the White House's history. She collected furnishings of past presidents and redecorated the mansion with these items.
Barbara Bush—Barbara Bush worked very hard to increase literacy in America.

Page 54
1. popcorn
2. oldest
3. Peru
4. calories
5. oil
6. religious
7. Nebraska
8. popcorn
9. outer
10. pressure
11. peanuts
12. inside
13. nutrients
14. Mexico
15. oldest
16. not
17. television
18. Hemisphere

Bonus Box answer: Popcorn Poppin Month

Page 56

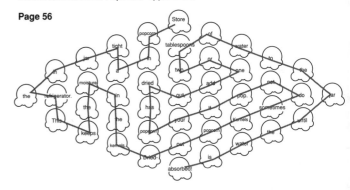

Page 58

	ballerina	ghost	cheer-leader	scare-crow	magician	soccer player
Malorie	✓	✗	✗	✗	✗	✗
Jimmy	✗	✗	✗	✗	✗	✓
Hanna	✗	✗	✓	✗	✗	✗
Christopher	✗	✗	✗	✓	✗	✗
John	✗	✗	✗	✗	✓	✗
Michael	✗	✓	✗	✗	✗	✗

Malorie—5
Jimmy—3
Hanna—1
Christopher—6
John—2
Michael—4

Page 59
1. Dr. Jekyll
2. Wanda Witch
3. Uma Alien
4. Mike Monster
5. Ben Bit
6. Stephen King
7. Count Dracula
8. Mr. Hyde
9. Terror Trail
10. Alfred Hitchcock
11. Dracula Drive
12. Francis Fear

Riddle answer: "You Are So 'Bootiful' To Me!"

Page 62
1. north
2. west
3. south
4. Bonz house
5. south
6. west
7. Ghoul house
8. east
9. Ghost house
10. west
11. east

64